BRIDGE CONVENTIONS IN DEPTH

MATTHEW & PAMELA GRANOVETTER

MASTER POINT PRESS

TORONTO

Master Point Press

331 Douglas Ave.
Toronto, Ontario Canada
M5M 1H2
(416) 781-0351 Fax (416) 781-1831
Internet www.masterpointpress.com

Canadian Cataloguing in Publication Data

Granovetter, Matthew
Bridge Conventions in depth/ Matthew and Pamela Granovetter.

ISBN 1-894154-56-8
ISBN 978-1-894154-56-7

1. Contract bridge — Bidding. I. Granovetter, Pamela, 1946 — II. Title.
GV1282.4.G72 2003   795.41'52   C2003-900086-9

Editor   Ray Lee
Cover and interior design   Olena S. Sullivan/New Mediatrix
Interior format and copyediting   Deanna Bourassa

Printed and bound in Canada by Webcom Canada Ltd.

2 3 4 5 6 7   10 09 08 07 06

CONTENTS

How many times have you decided to play a convention and then found when it came up that you still had no idea what to do? The main purpose of this book is to present conventions *in depth*, giving readers and partnerships a thorough understanding of how to continue to get the most out of a convention after the conventional bid has been made.

We think conventions are fun! But only if the partnership is on the same wavelength about what they mean. It's easy to say, 'Let's play Jacoby transfers,' then write it on the convention card and start playing. But suddenly it comes up and you want to know how to make a quantitative bid describing a slam invitation with a five-card major. Are you sure partner will read your subsequent jump to 4NT as not forcing?

We hope you'll take what you like from the book and use it in your own partnerships. You won't find here a study of all existing conventions. Instead, you'll find an interesting selection of conventions, which we particularly enjoy playing and find useful. Most of these conventions are 'add-ons'. They can be added to your card without disturbing the rest of your system. Some go way back to our rubber bridge and cut-around-IMP days at the old Mayfair and Cavendish Clubs in New York. Most come from the tournament world in our discussions with various champions. Some are not exactly conventions but simply nuances, 'state secrets', used until now only by a select few top-level partnerships.

Enjoy!

Matthew and Pamela Granovetter

BASIC CONVENTIONS - THE REST OF THE STORY

PART ONE

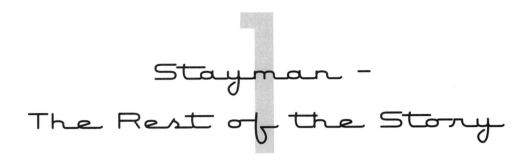

PREVIEW

Your partner opens the bidding with one notrump (15 to a bad 18) and you hold:

♠ K 8 3 2   ♡   A 4   ◇   A J 10 3   ♣ K 6 4

Partner	You
1NT	2♣
2♠	?

Do you have any idea what to bid next?

THE SOLUTION

In real life, the player with this hand bid 4♣, meaning it as Gerber. His partner thought it was a splinter, showing a singleton, and got very excited with:

♠ A 7 5 4   ♡   K Q J   ◇   K Q 4   ♣ J 3 2

Partner checked for keycards, found out your hand had three without the queen of spades, and screeched to a halt in five spades. The good news was that there was only one club loser, but the bad news was that the spades broke 4-1. The whole deal:

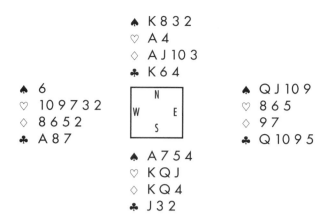

```
                    ♠ K 8 3 2
                    ♡ A 4
                    ◇ A J 10 3
                    ♣ K 6 4
    ♠ 6                           ♠ Q J 10 9
    ♡ 10 9 7 3 2      N           ♡ 8 6 5
    ◇ 8 6 5 2     W       E       ◇ 9 7
    ♣ A 8 7           S           ♣ Q 10 9 5
                    ♠ A 7 5 4
                    ♡ K Q J
                    ◇ K Q 4
                    ♣ J 3 2
```

We can't really say that North-South were unlucky because with these cards they already needed some luck to make four spades.

Is there any way North-South can make a slam investigation without going past game? Yes, there is!

After Stayman and the response of a major by the opening notrump bidder, a bid of three of the other major shows slam interest in opener's major.

Opener	Responder
1NT	2♣
2♡	3♠[1]

1. Slam interest in hearts, usually a balanced hand.

Opener	Responder
1NT	2♣
2♠	3♡[1]

1. Slam interest in spades, usually a balanced hand.

Opener	Responder
2NT	3♣
3♡	3♠[1]

1. Slam try in hearts.

Opener	Responder
2NT	3♣
3♠	4♡[1]

1. Slam try in spades.

In the fourth example auction, responder is unable to bid the other major at the three-level, so he must bid 4♡. This leaves very little room for investigating, but it is better than nothing and is consistent with the other three auctions.

In our original example, the opening bidder, with his 4-3-3-3 minimum hand, has no interest in slam. However, suppose the hands are:

Opener	Responder
♠ A Q J 5	♠ K 8 3 2
♡ J 3 2	♡ A 4
◇ K Q 6 5	◇ A J 10 3
♣ A 2	♣ K 6 4

This time the opener has a maximum in point count, great trumps and a doubleton. The bidding goes:

Opener	Responder
1NT	2♣
2♠	3♡[1]
4♣	4NT[2]
5♠[3]	6♠

1. Slam try in spades, usually balanced.
2. Controls everywhere, so he takes over.
3. Two keycards plus the queen of trumps.

Since responder can set the trump suit by bidding three of the other major, there is no confusion about:

Opener	Responder
1NT	2♣
2♠	4NT

This is clearly quantitative (with four hearts); if you like spades and want to launch into Blackwood, bid 3♡ first, agreeing spades, then bid 4NT next round.

These 'other major' bids also apply after a 2NT opening:

Opener	Responder
2NT	3♣
3♡	3♠[1]

1. Hearts, slam try.

Opener	Responder
2NT	3♣
3♠	4♡[1]

1. Spades, slam try.

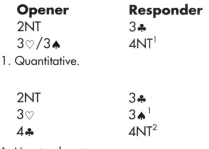
Opener	Responder
2NT	3♣
3♡/3♠	4NT[1]

1. Quantitative.

Opener	Responder
2NT	3♣
3♡	3♠[1]
4♣	4NT[2]

1. Hearts, slam try.
2. Blackwood.

What about the sequence we started off with, where responder jumped to the four-level?

Opener	Responder
1NT	2♣
2♠	4♣/4◇/4♡

It's useful to play these jumps to a new suit as splinters. But a word of caution: a splinter bid should promise reasonable trumps (we suggest Q10xx or better). By jumping to the four-level, you take up lots of investigation-room, and may end up in a poor slam, such as on these hands:

Opener	Responder
♠ A 7 6 5	♠ Q 8 3 2
♡ A J 8 4	♡ 9
◇ K 7	◇ A Q J 4 2
♣ K J 10	♣ A Q 4

1NT	2♣
2♠	4♡
?	

Slam looks like a good bet from the notrump bidder's perspective, so opener checked for key-cards and bid a slam. This slam was less than 50%, however, because in addition to needing the king of spades onside, North-South needed a 3-2 spade break. It didn't work out that way and they went down a trick.

What should responder do? Conscious of his weak trumps, he should go slowly:

Opener	Responder
♠ A 7 6 5	♠ Q 8 3 2
♡ A J 8 4	♡ 9
◇ K 7	◇ A Q J 4 2
♣ K J 10	♣ A Q 4

Opener	Responder
1NT	2♣
2♠	3♡[1]
4♣	4♢
4♡	5♠[2]
pass[3]	

1. Slam try in spades, usually with a balanced hand.
2. How good are your trumps?
3. Not so good.

The whole deal was:

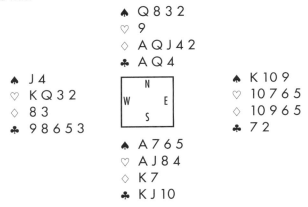

♠ Q 8 3 2
♡ 9
♢ A Q J 4 2
♣ A Q 4

♠ J 4   ♠ K 10 9
♡ K Q 3 2   ♡ 10 7 6 5
♢ 8 3   ♢ 10 9 6 5
♣ 9 8 6 5 3   ♣ 7 2

♠ A 7 6 5
♡ A J 8 4
♢ K 7
♣ K J 10

Notice that if we improve the trump spots, the slam makes:

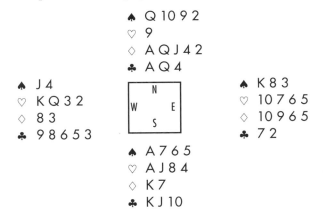

♠ Q 10 9 2
♡ 9
♢ A Q J 4 2
♣ A Q 4

♠ J 4   ♠ K 8 3
♡ K Q 3 2   ♡ 10 7 6 5
♢ 8 3   ♢ 10 9 6 5
♣ 9 8 6 5 3   ♣ 7 2

♠ A 7 6 5
♡ A J 8 4
♢ K 7
♣ K J 10

Now the auction would proceed like this:

South	North
1NT	2♣
2♠	4♡[1]
4NT	5♠[2]
6♠	

1. Splinter bid.
2. Two keycards plus the queen of trumps.

South got the ♡K lead, won the ace, played a club to the queen, and led the queen of trumps off dummy. Had the queen lost to the king, he would win the next lead in dummy and finesse for the jack of spades on his right. What a difference the spots make!

Here are some more misunderstandings that frequently occur after Stayman:

1. **If opener responds 2♢, what does two-of-a-major by responder mean?**

Opener	Responder
1NT	2♣
2♢	2♡ or 2♠

2. **If opener responds with a major, what does the bid of a minor suit by responder mean? How forcing is it?**

Opener	Responder
1NT	2♣
2♠	3♣

3. **If opener has both majors, which should he bid first?**

4. **Can opener have a five-card major? If so, how does he show it?**

OUR SUGGESTIONS

1. **If opener responds 2♢, what does two-of-a-major by responder mean?**

Opener	Responder
1NT	2♣
2♢	2♡ or 2♠

We do not bid Stayman with a very weak hand and four-four or five-four in the majors, at least as a partnership agreement (we may decide to do this at favorable vulnerability, but partner will not play us for it). We simply transfer to the five-card major and leave it at that.

Opener	Responder
1NT	2♣
2◇ or 2♡	2♠[1]

1. Five spades, a shade too weak to transfer and then bid 2NT.

Opener	Responder
1NT	2♣
2◇	2♡[1]

1. Five hearts and four spades, a shade too weak for Smolen.

(The excellent Smolen convention shows five-four in the majors and a game force. You bid Stayman, and if your partner responds with 2◇, you jump in your four-card major. Partner will convert to your five-card major with three of them, or rebid 3NT without. Works over a 2NT opening bid as well, except that you don't jump. For a full description, see Part 2.)

2. If opener responds with a major, what does the bid of a minor suit by responder mean? How forcing is it?

Opener	Responder
1NT	2♣
2♠	3♣

For simplicity, the new suit is forcing to game. The above auction shows four hearts, five clubs and a game force, although you could have four spades and five clubs, planning next to bid 4♠ as a natural slam try (e.g., ♠KQxx ♡xx ◇xx ♣AKJxx).

3. If opener has both majors, which should he bid first?
There should not be a hard-and-fast rule for this. You should use your judgment. If your spades are AKxx and your hearts are Jxxx, you should bid spades first. Perhaps the hand is something like this:

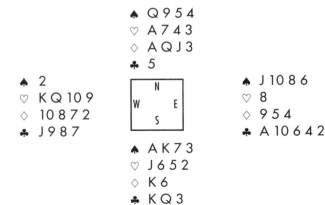

In four spades, you can stand the bad trump break; in four hearts you cannot. When the deal actually occurred, West led the ♡K against 4♠. Declarer won the ace and cashed three rounds of trumps. Next he played four rounds of diamonds, pitching two hearts. East gave it his best shot by refusing to ruff the fourth diamond, winning the ace of clubs and playing the last trump. Declarer would have been short a trick had his clubs been KJx instead of KQx.

4. Can opener have a five-card major? If so, how does he show it?

Yes, but opener should be careful. Suppose he has five spades and two hearts, and responder has three spades and five hearts. Responder transfers to hearts and then bids 3NT. Now you're playing 3NT instead of your 5-3 spade fit. Therefore, if you open 1NT with five in a major, you should always have 3 cards in the other major. Here's what can happen if you don't follow this rule:

Opener	Responder
♠ A 9	♠ K Q 8 7 2
♡ K Q 7 6 2	♡ A J 3
◇ J 5 4	◇ 3 2
♣ A Q 3	♣ J 8 4

1NT	2♡[1]
2♠	3NT
pass	

1. Transfer.

The opponents take the first five diamond tricks; meanwhile you are cold for 4♡. But if you have three spades along with your five-card heart suit, you are safe:

Opener	Responder
♠ A 9 4	♠ K Q 8 7 2
♡ K Q 7 6 2	♡ A J 3
◇ J 5 4	◇ 3 2
♣ A Q	♣ J 8 4

1NT	2♡[1]
2♠	3NT
4♠	

1. Transfer.

If you've opened 1NT with a five-card major and partner bids Stayman, jump to three of your suit. Again, you do not want to miss that 5-3 fit.

Opener	Responder
♠ A 9 4	♠ K Q 8 7
♡ K Q 7 6 2	♡ A J 3
◇ J 3	◇ 5 4
♣ A Q J	♣ 8 4 3 2
1NT	2♣
3♡	4♡

Jacoby Transfers – The Rest of the Story

Jacoby Transfers are today a basic part of most people's bidding arsenal. After an opening bid of 1NT or 2NT, responder can transfer to a major at the cheapest level:

In response to 1NT:
2♢ = transfer to hearts
2♡ = transfer to spades

In response to an opening 2NT:
3♢ = transfer to hearts
3♡ = transfer to spades

After the transfer, responder is well-placed to pass with a weak hand, invite game with 2NT or three of the major, show a second suit, or offer a choice of games by bidding 3NT. The biggest advantage of transfers is to force the stronger hand to declare.

Here are some questions that you may not have thought about, however:

1. **Can opener bid something other than the transfer suit?**

2. **What are the implications when responder shows a second suit? Is this forcing? A slam try?**

3. **What does it mean if responder jump-shifts after the transfer, for example:**

Opener	Responder
1NT	2◇[1]
2♡	4♣[2]

    1. Transfer to hearts.
    2. ?

4. **What does 4NT mean after the transfer? How does responder ask for aces (or key-cards in his transfer suit)?**

5. **What happens if the opponent doubles the transfer?**

Partner	Oppt	You	Oppt
1NT	pass	2◇	dbl
?			

6. **Are transfers on in competition? For example:**

Partner	Oppt	You	Oppt
1NT	2♣	?	

7. **What does it mean if responder bids the other major at the three- or four-level? For example:**

Opener	Responder
1NT	2♡[1]
2♠	3♡ or 4♡

    1. Transfer to spades.

1. Can opener bid something other than the transfer suit?

Opener can jump to the three-level with four-card support and a maximum hand, a hand on which the partnership might miss game if responder passes the transfer at the two-level. (In recent years, other bids have been added to the repertoire here, such as the bid of a new suit to show a doubleton and a maximum with four trumps. This has some validity, but we don't like the modern tendency to bid past the transfer suit with fewer than four trumps or less than a maximum notrump, because you often get overboard when responder is weak.)

2. What are the implications when responder shows a second suit? Is this forcing? A slam try?

A second suit should be forcing to game, but not necessarily a slam-try. Responder, with two suits, simply wants to play the best game. An example:

♠ A 9 6 4 3   ♡ 4   ◇ K Q 4 3   ♣ 6 5 3

Here you transfer to spades and rebid 3◇. Without this agreement, you are forced to transfer to 2♠, and then bid 3NT. With a doubleton spade, partner might pass and you could miss the good five-diamond game, for example, if partner holds:

♠ J 4   ♡ A 9 7 5   ◇ A J 9 6   ♣ A K 8

On these cards, partner has a maximum, but three notrump hasn't much play, while five diamonds is a good bet.

3. What does it mean if responder jump-shifts after the transfer, for example:

Opener	Responder
1NT	2◇[1]
2♡	4♣[2]

1. Transfer to hearts.

The popular idea is to play the second-round jump shift as showing a singleton and six cards or more in your suit (you are forcing your side to play in your major, after all). An alternative is to play the jump shift as artificial, using 4♣ as a slam try with a weak major suit, and 4◇ as a slam try with a strong suit.

4. What does 4NT mean after the transfer? How does responder ask for aces (or key-cards in his transfer suit)?

After the transfer, in standard bidding 4NT now is quantitative. You have shown 15-16 high-card points with a five-card major and no second suit. How do you ask for aces? You make a Texas Transfer and then bid 4NT (see page 16).

Basic Conventions

5. What happens if the opponent doubles the transfer?

Partner	Oppt	You	Oppt
1NT	pass	2◇	dbl
?			

The standard treatment is to play that accepting the transfer after the double (by bidding 2♡ here, for example) shows three or more trumps, and passing shows two trumps.

6. Are transfers on in competition? For example:

Partner	Oppt	You	Oppt
1NT	2♣	?	

Transfers are not 'on' in competition (unless you and your partner have some special agreement on this -- for example, some play that if 2♣ was artificial, a double is Stayman and transfers are on). Your bid at the two-level is natural and to play, but you can transfer at the three-level (see page 184).

7. What does it mean if responder bids the other major at the three- or four-level?

For example:

Opener	Responder
1NT	2♡[1]
2♠	3♡ or 4♡

1. Transfer to spades.

Normally, a transfer to spades followed by a heart bid shows 5-5 in the majors (with 5-4 distribution, start with Stayman rather than a transfer), forcing to game. A 4♡ jump after a transfer to spades also shows 5-5 in the majors, but is a slam try. However, if you prefer, you can play the 4♡ bid to show a singleton heart and six spades, and the 3♡ bid can show 5-5 in the majors, game-forcing, possibly a slam try. Similarly, a transfer to hearts followed by a jump to 3♠ can be used to show either a 6-5 hand or a singleton spade (it's up to you and your partner to decide which you prefer).

Bridge Conventions in Depth

Texas Transfers – The Rest of the Story

Just like Jacoby Transfers, Texas Transfers are played over both 1NT and 2NT openings. A direct response of 4◇ or 4♡ is a transfer to the next higher suit and shows at least a six-card suit.

Opener	Responder
1NT or 2NT	4◇ = transfer to 4♡
	4♡ = transfer to 4♠

After 1NT, Texas Transfers are sign-offs, and you will pass the forced response in your major suit. The exception is when you were simply using Texas to set your major as trumps, in which case after partner accepts the transfer, you bid 4NT, Blackwood (or Keycard Blackwood).

Opener	Responder
♠ A K 7	♠ Q 10 8 6 5 3 2
♡ Q 5	♡ 10 9 4
◇ A 10 8 3	◇ 5 2
♣ Q 7 6 2	♣ 8

Opener	Responder
1NT	4♡[1]
4♠	pass

1. Transfer to spades.

In this case, responder's Texas Transfer bid is essentially a preempt. The whole deal:

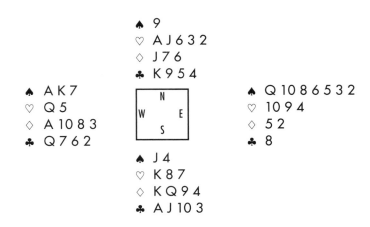

	♠ 9		
	♡ A J 6 3 2		
	◇ J 7 6		
	♣ K 9 5 4		

West	North	East	South
♠ A K 7		♠ Q 10 8 6 5 3 2	
♡ Q 5		♡ 10 9 4	
◇ A 10 8 3		◇ 5 2	
♣ Q 7 6 2		♣ 8	

	♠ J 4		
	♡ K 8 7		
	◇ K Q 9 4		
	♣ A J 10 3		

West	**North**	**East**	**South**
1NT	pass	4♡[1]	pass
4♠	all pass		

1. Transfer to spades.

North-South wuz robbed! They comfortably make 5♡, but never got into the bidding.

Texas followed by 4NT is Blackwood, but as we have seen, Jacoby followed by 4NT is quantitative (a 5-3-3-2 shaped 15-16-count). Thus, by using Texas Transfers you can bid Blackwood (or Keycard Blackwood for your own suit). This is useful if you pick up a hand like:

♠ K Q 10 6 5 3 2   ♡ A 10 9   ◇ K 2   ♣ 8

Opener	**Responder**
1NT	4♡[1]
4♠	4NT[2]

1. Transfer to spades.
2. Blackwood (or Keycard Blackwood).

Texas can also be used to set up Exclusion Keycard Blackwood:

♠ K Q 10 6 5 3 2   ♡ A 10 9   ◇ K Q 2   ♣ —

Opener	**Responder**
1NT	4♡[1]
4♠	5♣[2]

1. Transfer to spades.
2. A new suit by responder shows a void, asking partner to respond
   to Blackwood excluding the ace of the void-suit (see 'Exclusion
   Blackwood', page 204.)

Thus, the Texas bidder can be very weak, very strong, or somewhere in between. If you think you can make a game, but you do not have a slam-try, you bid Texas and then pass partner's acceptance. Since you could be very weak, opener can never do anything other than accept the Texas Transfer, even when he holds a great hand for the bidding.

TEXAS IN COMPETITION

Over 1NT, a bid of 4♢ or 4♡ must be a jump-shift to be Texas. Therefore:

Partner	Oppt	You	Oppt
	1NT	2♠	4♢[1]

1. Texas transfer to hearts.

Partner	Oppt	You	Oppt
	1NT	3♠	4♢[1]

1. Natural, forcing.

Texas is 'on' after a double:

Partner	Oppt	You	Oppt
	1NT	dbl	4♢/4♡[1]

1. Texas transfer.

Jacoby Transfer followed by a raise to game vs. a Texas Transfer
Alert: the following idea applies only after a 2NT opening (not a 1NT opening).
You hold:

♠ A 4   ♡ Q 8 7 5 4 2   ♢ 8   ♣ Q J 7 6

Partner opens 2NT. What do you bid? And what is the difference between these two sequences:

a) Texas Transfer

Partner	You
2NT	4♢[1]
4♡	pass

1. Transfer to hearts.

b) Jacoby Transfer followed by a raise to game

Partner	You
2NT	3♢[1]
3♡	4♡

1. Transfer to hearts.

One of the two should be a slam try, whereas the other should be a weak hand with no interest. There is also a third type of hand, a hand with only a little interest in slam (i.e., if partner has a magic fit). You can use Texas for the first, where you have definite slam interest, and a Jacoby Transfer on both the other two hands. In the latter case, you will sign off in four of your major whatever partner does when you have a weak hand; if you find partner has the magic fit, then you can make another move on the right hand.

Let's designate Texas as the slam try after a 2NT opener. Your hand (above) was:

♠ A 4   ♡ Q 8 7 5 4 2   ◇ 8   ♣ Q J 7 6

Should you make a Texas transfer with this hand? You do have a little slam interest, although you wish your hearts were better. You are surely too good to merely transfer and then sign off in game, aren't you?

This is actually the third hand type. You bid 3◇, transfer to hearts. If your partner has good heart support and some controls, he bids 4♡. Otherwise you just raise 3♡ to 4♡ (denying a 'real' slam try).

For example:

Partner	You
♠ K Q J 4	♠ A 3
♡ K 9	♡ Q 8 7 5 4 2
◇ A K Q 4	◇ 8
♣ K 9 3	♣ Q J 7 6
2NT	3◇[1]
3♡	4♡

1. Transfer to hearts.

or

Partner	You
♠ K Q 9 4	♠ A 3
♡ A K 9	♡ Q 8 7 5 4 2
◇ A J 4	◇ 8
♣ A 9 3	♣ Q J 7 6
2NT	3◇[1]
4♡[2]	4NT[3]

1. Transfer to hearts.
2. Good hearts, good controls.
3. Blackwood.

What does a 'real' slam try look like? Mainly, your suit should play for one loser opposite ace, king, or queen doubleton. For example, bid Texas over a 2NT opener on any of these hands:

♠ A 4   ♡ Q J 10 5 4 2   ◇ 8   ♣ Q 8 7 6

♠ A 4   ♡ K J 10 5 4 2   ◇ 8   ♣ J 10 7 6

♠ K 4   ♡ A Q 8 7 5 4   ◇ 8 6   ♣ 8 7 6

Partner should accept your slam try with a maximum 2NT and nice controls. Trumps are not the issue.

Note: Remember, Texas has a different meaning after a one-notrump opening bid than it does after a two-notrump opening bid. It is a sign-off unless responder chooses to bid on. So if you want to try for slam, go through Jacoby and raise to game.

Over a 1NT opening:

Opener	Responder
1NT	2◇ [1]
2♡	4♡ [2]

1. Transfer to hearts.
2. Slam try.

Opener	Responder
1NT	4◇ [1]

1. Transfer to hearts, and a sign off.

But over a 2NT opening:

Opener	Responder
2NT	3◇ [1]
3♡	4♡ [2]

1. Transfer to hearts.
2. Sign off.

Opener	Responder
2NT	4◇ [1]

1. Transfer to hearts and a slam try.

Reverses – The Rest of the Story

Reverses aren't really a convention as such, but they are an important part of natural bidding. First, let's define a reverse:

Opener's Reverse is a rebid at the two-level in a new suit that ranks above his first-bid suit but below responder's.

Opener	Responder
1♢	1♠
2♡	

In this particular auction, 2♡ is the only available reverse.

Opener	Responder
1♣	1♠
2♢/2♡	

Here 2♢ and 2♡ are both reverses. A reverse shows 17+ points in strength, often with a fit for responder's suit. Everyone 'plays' reverses, but few partnerships discuss what happens after the reverse bid. The easiest way to play is:

1. **Reverses are forcing one round. Even if responder scraped up his first response on a minimum hand, he must bid again over the reverse.** The reverse may have been made on a three-card suit if opener was stuck (see point #2, below).

2. **Responder's first obligation is to rebid a five-card major.** Opener's reverse might have been made on a three-card suit because he has strong three-card support for responder, but is stuck for a bid. For example: opener holds

    ♠ A K 5   ♡ 8 6   ♢ A 5 2   ♣ A K 9 6 3

The bidding goes:

Opener	Responder
1♣	1♠
?	

Opener cannot jump to 3♠ or 4♠ with only three spades. The right contract might be in notrump or clubs, and it is foolish to blast into a spade game, possibly playing in a 4-3 fit, going down, when other contracts are superior.

What about a 2NT rebid, certainly the value bid? Opener hates to rebid two notrump with two small hearts. If notrump is the right game, it should be played from the other side: opener has no tenaces and no stopper in hearts.

Suppose you do rebid 2NT, and partner raises to 3NT. They lead the ♡Q and dummy arrives with something like:

♠ Q J 7 6   ♡ K 4 2   ◇ 7 4 3   ♣ Q 8 4

You are going to feel ridiculous going down in three notrump from your side, when ten tricks are odds-on from partner's side.

Let's go back to opener's rebid problem.

♠ A K 5   ♡ 8 6   ◇ A 5 2   ♣ A K 9 6 3

The bidding goes:

Opener	Responder
1♣	1♠
?	

What opener wants to know is: (a) Does partner have five spades? (b) If not, does partner have a heart stopper?

Opener can discover this information by bidding 2◇, a reverse, which is forcing for one round. Responder must, therefore, go out of his way to rebid his five-card spade suit (there's one exception to this, which we'll get to in just a moment). Bidding notrump, or supporting opener's first suit, can wait.

3. If responder does not have a five-card major to rebid, he bids as follows:

a) With a very weak hand, responder warns partner that he is going to pass at his next bid. He does this by bidding either the fourth suit at the two-level or 2NT (whichever is cheaper). This does not guarantee a weak hand — it simply alerts opener to the possibility:

Opener	Responder
1♣	1♠
2◇	2♡

Here 2♡ will be either a very weak hand, planning to pass opener's next bid (♠QJxxx ♡Qxx ◇xxx ♣xx — scraped up a 1♠ response, but too weak to show the 5-card suit);

natural (♠QJxxx ♡Axxx ◇xx ♣Qx); or a fourth-suit forcing catch-all, i.e., a game-going hand but nothing to rebid (for instance QJxx Jxx KQx xxx).

Opener	Responder
1◇	1♠
2♡	2NT

Here either 2NT is natural, or responder is planning to pass opener's next bid.

Therefore, after a reverse, the partnership can stop comfortably in a partscore:

Opener	Responder
1♣	1♠
2◇	2♡[1]
2♠	pass

1. Fourth suit at the two-level — responder may be planning to pass next time.

Opener	Responder
1◇	1♠
2♡	2NT[1]
3◇	pass

1. Fourth suit not available at the two-level.

b) Responder can show support for opener and a game-forcing hand at the same time.

Opener	Responder
1♣	1♠
2◇	3♣[1]

1. Responder has club support and a hand worth a game force e.g.

♠ Q J 7 3　♡ J 8 2　◇ K 4　♣ Q 7 6 5

Opener	Responder
1♣	1♠
2◇	4♣[1]

1. Responder has great club support and slam interest e.g.

♠ Q J 7 3　♡ A 2　◇ K Q 4　♣ Q J 6 5

Opener	Responder
1♣	1♠
2◇	3♡[1]

1. This shows 5-5 in the majors, and is game-forcing.

Opener	Responder
1♣	1♠
2♢	3♠[1]

1. Responder has a strong 6-card spade suit.

Opener	Responder
1♣	1♠
2♢	3♢[1]

1. A natural raise, probably with 5-4 shape.

Opener	Responder
1♣	1♠
2♢	3NT[1]

1. Since 2NT here is game-forcing (2♡ is available for the weak hand), 3NT shows extras and is a mild slam try e.g.

♠ Q J 6 2   ♡ A K 4   ♢ K 7 5   ♣ 5 4 2

Weak Jump Shifts — The Rest of the Story

The immediate jump shift by responder is traditionally a strong bid, but many partnerships today play weak jump shifts, showing a six-card or longer suit and less than 7 points. This agreement works especially well with 2/1 methods, since the need for the strong jump shift is largely removed by the game-forcing nature of the initial 2/1 response.

The method we recommend is called **3/4 Weak Jump Shifts**. In this scheme, the weak jump shift does not apply to a passed hand if the opponents aren't in the bidding (we assume that the passed hand would have already opened the bidding with a preempt if he had one — though there are occasions when you cannot). But it does apply when you're a passed hand and there's an overcall or double by your RHO — for example:

Partner	Oppt	You	Oppt
		pass	pass
1◇	1♡	?	

Now a jump shift is weak. So the 3/4 means that it's on when you're an unpassed hand or whenever there's an overcall or takeout double.

Examples of weak jump shift auctions:

Opener	Responder
1♣	2◇, 2♡ or 2♠

Opener	Responder
1◇	2♡, 2♠, or 3♣

Opener	Responder
1♡	2♠, 3♣, or 3◇

Opener	Responder
1♠	3♣, 3◇ or 3♡

The two main advantages of playing weak jump shifts are:

1. **They preempt LHO, taking up his bidding space;**

2. **They describe your hand in one bid and make it easier to reach game when you hit partner with the right hand.**

The value of preempting is obvious: your LHO, especially when he's fourth to bid, cannot make a bid with a hand worth only a minimum overcall:

West	North	East	South
1♣	pass	2♡	?

Suppose South holds something like:

♠ A K J 6 3   ♡ 5 4 3   ◇ 8 6 2   ♣ 6 5

If East responds one heart, South can slip in a lead-directing 1♠ bid. After the jump to 2♡, South is forced either to pass or to overstate his values.

Here's another advantage. Playing weak jump shift responses, opener can distinguish between partner's very weak hand with a 6-card suit, and a stronger minimum hand with a 6-card suit:

Opener	Responder
1♣	2♡

Opener	Responder
1♣	1♡
1♠	2♡

In the second auction, opener knows that responder holds 7-9 HCP and a six-card suit. Opener can now make a game try with a good hand for his partner:

♠ A Q 5 2   ♡ K   ◇ 7 6 3   ♣ A K 6 5 4

Opener	Responder
1♣	1♡
1♠	2♡
3♡	

Basic Conventions

♠ Q 6 5 2   ♡ A 4   ◇ 7 6   ♣ A K Q 5 4

Opener	Responder
1♣	1♡
1♠	2♡
3♡	

♠ Q J 9 6   ♡ K 4   ◇ A Q 6   ♣ K Q J 5

Opener	Responder
1♣	1♡
1♠	2♡
2NT	

On this hand, you don't know whether to play in 3NT or 4♡. Suppose opposite each of these hands partner holds:

♠ K 4   ♡ Q J 10 6 5 2   ◇ K 2   ♣ 8 7 3

Now partner bids 4♡ over the 3♡ game try, and 3NT over the 2NT bid (4♡ might go down on a club ruff).

GAME TRIES OVER THE WJS

Opener can make a game try after the weak jump response by bidding 2NT, which is forcing:

Opener	Responder
1♣	2♡
2NT	?

Responder can answer with the Modified Ogust steps (see page 61), although the maximum will be much weaker than the maximum for a weak-two bid:

3♣ = the worst

♠ Q 6   ♡ J 10 9 8 4 3   ◇ 6 5 2   ♣ 7 2

3◇ = maximum

♠ 6   ♡ Q J 10 8 4 3   ◇ K 6 5   ♣ 7 4 2

3♡ = good suit, bad hand

♠ 6 2   ♡ Q J 10 8 4 3   ◇ Q 6 5   ♣ 7 2

3♠ = natural

♠ J 6 3 2   ♡ A J 9 8 4 3   ◇ 6 5   ♣ 2

Bridge Conventions in Depth

3NT = 2 of the top 3 honors

♠ 6 2   ♡ A Q 8 5 4 3   ◊ 6 5 2   ♣ 7 2

If opener has:

♠ A K 5   ♡ K 7 6 2   ◊ 4   ♣ A K Q 6 5

he would be looking for at least game and maybe slam!

Opener signs off in game after the 3♣ response. Over the 3◊ and 3♡ responses he would use Blackwood and stop in 5♡ on finding out about the missing two aces. He would use Blackwood and go on to slam opposite our example hands for the 3♠ and 3NT responses.

Without the weak jump shift conventions, on all these hands the auction would usually go:

Opener	Responder
1♣	1♡
4◊ [1]	4♡

1. Splinter

and some of the time, an excellent slam would be missed.

Drury – The Rest of the Story

A Canadian invention that has become part of everyday life, like the telephone, the Drury convention is a passed-hand 2♣ response to a major-suit opening.

West	North	East	South
	pass	pass	1♡ or 1♠
pass	2♣		

Drury is used on invitational hands and is designed to allow the partnership to stop at the two-level when third hand has a light opener or only a four-card major. When this bid was introduced to the duplicate world many years ago, it meant that responder had 10 or more points and either clubs or support for partner's major.

Nowadays, the bid usually promises at least three-card trump support and says nothing about clubs. Instead, a jump to 3♣ shows six clubs and 10-11 points, without support for opener's major.

In the original version of Drury, the opener rebids 2♢ to say he has a light opening bid, and the auction proceeds naturally from there. Responder can even introduce a five-card heart suit:

West	North	East	South
pass	pass	1♠	pass
2♣[1]	pass	2♢[2]	pass
2♡[3]			

1. Drury.
2. Light hand.
3. Natural, not forcing, typically three spades and five hearts.

If East opened the bidding on a weak hand with four spades and three hearts, he can pass and East-West can play in their 8-card heart fit instead of their 7-card spade fit.

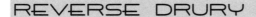
REVERSE DRURY

This very popular modern variation reverses the meanings of opener's rebids. If opener has a sound opening bid, he rebids 2◇, while any other rebid shows a light opening.

TWO-WAY DRURY

Another variation is to play the 2♣ response to the major-suit opening to show three trumps and a 2◇ response to show four trumps. The disadvantage here is that you lose the natural 2◇ response to the major-suit opening, as well as the natural 2♣ response.

DRURY IN COMPETITION

Some people play Drury even when the 1♡ opening is overcalled with 1♠ or when there is a takeout double.

If you play frequent four-card-majors in third and fourth seat (see page 57), it's important to play Drury the old-fashioned way, i.e., to show either clubs or three-card support, forcing one round, because opener may have four clubs and only a four-card major and a normal 3♣ contract on a 5-4 fit could be missed. Here's a horrible example of what can happen without that understanding:

♠ A 7 5 3	♠ 6 2
♡ 5 3 2	♡ Q 8
◇ A Q	◇ K 6 5 4
♣ J 9 7 4	♣ A Q 10 6 2

Opener	Responder
	pass
1♠	1NT
pass	

The defense took the first five heart tricks and then switched to spades. When the club finesse lost, declarer finished down three.

OPENER'S REBIDS AFTER DRURY

Playing old-fashioned Drury, a 1♠ opener's responses are:

2◇	=	natural, or minimum hand with 4 spades
2♡	=	natural (5+ spades, 4+ hearts)
2♠	=	minimum, 5 spades
2NT	=	natural, forcing
3♣	=	natural, forcing

This is how the auction should go on that last example:

♠ A 7 5 3	♠ 6 2
♡ 5 3 2	♡ Q 8
◇ A Q	◇ K 6 5 4
♣ J 9 7 4	♣ A Q 10 6 2

Opener	Responder
	pass
1♠	2♣
2◇[1]	2NT[2]
3♣[3]	pass

1. Natural, or minimum hand with 4 spades.
2. Denies spade support, ergo he has clubs.
3. He has denied a full opening bid with clubs (he did not raise 2♣ to 3♣), ergo he has club support without a full opening bid.

Suppose you hold:

♠ 5 3 ♡ K Q 6 ◇ 7 6 5 ♣ A Q 7 4 2

You	Partner
pass	1♠
2♣	2♠
pass	

You should be safe playing the 5-2 fit at the two-level.

You	Partner
pass	1♠
2♣	3♣[1]
3♡	

1. Forcing.

Your heart bid doesn't promise a four- or five-card suit (though you could hold one). Once partner raises your clubs, you are going to game, but if the game is 3NT you prefer to play it from partner's side. Your 3♡ bid simply shows a stopper for notrump. Partner now bids 3NT, cold from his side, with:

♠ A 8 7 4 2 ♡ A 5 ◇ K 4 ♣ K 8 5 3

What if partner doesn't have a diamond stopper? If you have the same hand,

♠ 5 3 ♡ K Q 6 ◇ 7 6 5 ♣ A Q 7 4 2

the bidding might go:

You	Partner
pass	1♠
2♣	3♣
3♡	4♡
?	

You can bid 4♠ on your way to 5♣, just in case partner can play opposite your doubleton (you would have bid 3♠ over 3♣ with three-card spade support). If partner holds

♠ A K Q 6 2   ♡ J 10 4   ◇ 3   ♣ K 6 5 3

or

♠ A K Q 6 2   ♡ A 8 4   ◇ 3 2   ♣ J 10 5

he will pass 4♠, which offers a better chance for game than 5♣.

ANOTHER USE FOR THE 3♣ RESPONSE

Now that the two-club Drury response might be natural with clubs, you can use the 3♣ response by a passed hand to show a specific hand, for example:

a) **five clubs and a four-card fit for partner; or**
b) **a six-card club suit with three of the top four honors. A grand slam was once reached in a major tournament, using this agreement, when the auction went:**

Opener	Responder
	pass
1♠	3♣
7♣!	

The hands were:

Opener	Responder
♠ A K 8 7 5 3	♠ 6 2
♡ A J 6 4	♡ 7 3
◇ —	◇ Q 5 2
♣ Q 8 2	♣ A K J 7 6 3

WHEN NOT TO USE DRURY

With 12 HCP and four trumps, don't waste time with Drury; just raise partner's opening bid to the three- or four-level (depending on your hand). Drury could put too much pressure on partner:

Basic Conventions

Opener	Responder
♠ 10 7 5 3 2	♠ K Q J 4
♡ 6 5	♡ 7 4 3
◇ A Q J 6	◇ K 7 2
♣ A 4	♣ K 6 3

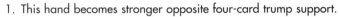

	pass
1♠	3♠
4♠[1]	

1. This hand becomes stronger opposite four-card trump support.

Here you chose to pass the 4-3-3-3 aceless 12-count, but now that partner has opened one spade, you must compensate. Dainty Drury bidding isn't enough because you know that partner will be worried about trumps and is unlikely to accept any game invitations.

The Grand Slam Force – The Rest of the Story

One of Ely Culbertson's contributions to bidding theory, the 5NT Grand Slam Force, was originally named 'Josephine' by him, after his wife and favorite bridge partner. Once a trump suit has been agreed, either specifically or by implication, jumping to 5NT asks partner to bid seven with two of the top three trump honors. This is the traditional meaning. Most partnerships also agree on some meaning for a suit response at the six-level below the trump suit.

Opener	Responder
1♡	3♡[1]
5NT	?

1. Limit raise.

6♣ = ace or king of trumps
6♢ = queen of trumps or extra length

So, in our example auction,

with ♡ Axxx or ♡ Kxxx, responder bids 6♣.
with ♡ Qxxx or ♡ xxxxx, responder bids 6♢.
with ♡ AKxx, ♡ AQxx, or ♡ KQxx, responder bids 7♡.

Over a 6♣ response, you can bid 6♢ to ask for extra trump length. For example:

Opener	Responder
♠ A K 4 3	♠ 8 7 6
♡ K 8 7 5 4	♡ A 9 6 3 2
◇ A K Q J	◇ 6 4
♣ —	♣ K Q 8

Opener	Responder
1♡	3♡
5NT	6♣[1]
6◇[2]	7♡[3]

1. Ace or king.
2. Asks for extra length.
3. Extra length.

USING 5NT AS A TRUMP ASKING BID

The 5NT Grand Slam Force can be used in a modified form when partner shows a long and strong suit. Here, the Grand Slam Force does not ask for two of the top three honors, but, rather, for solidity.

Opener	Responder
4♡	5NT
?	

In general, a jump to seven now shows a suit that will run even opposite a void, like ♡AKQJ7642. But what about bids at the six-level? Responses of 6♣ and 6◇ can be used to show hands that cannot play seven opposite a void, but can play opposite a singleton, doubleton, or tripleton, i.e.:

Opener	Responder
4♡	5NT
6♣	?

6♣ shows a solid suit opposite either a singleton or a doubleton; now the 5NT bidder bids 7♡ with a doubleton, or 6◇ with a singleton; with a void he signs off in 6♡.

Opener	Responder
4♡	5NT
6♣	6◇[1]
?	

1. I have a singleton trump.

With ♡AK76432, West signs off in six hearts. With ♡AKQ7643, he bids seven.

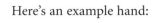

Here's an example hand:

Opener	Responder
♠ 9	♠ A 6 5
♡ A K 9 7 6 5 4 2	♡ 8
◇ J 8 7	◇ A 4
♣ J	♣ A K Q 6 5 4 3

Opener	Responder
4♡	5NT
6♣	6◇
6♡	pass

Here 6♣ said West was (probably) solid opposite either a singleton or doubleton trump. With only a singleton heart, East bids 6◇ and West signs off.

The other possible six-level response to 5NT is 6◇:

Opener	Responder
4♡	5NT
6◇	?

6◇ says that opener's suit is (probably) solid only opposite the queen, or three small trumps.

Here's an example of this sequence in action:

Opener	Responder
♠ J 8	♠ A 6
♡ A K 10 9 7 6 5	♡ 8 4 2
◇ J 8 7 2	◇ A 4
♣ ——	♣ A K Q J 5 4

Opener	Responder
4♡	5NT
6◇	7NT[1]
pass	

1. Opposite three small hearts opener's suit should play for seven tricks.

When the trump suit is clubs or diamonds, a jump to 5♡ or 5♠ can be used as the Grand Slam Force instead of 5NT, with the response steps moving down accordingly.

FISHING FOR ANOTHER SUIT

Many play the response of 7♣ to 5NT as showing two of the top three honors. The idea here is that the player who bids 5NT may hold a solid suit of his own and want to play in his own suit at the seven-level if partner's suit contains two of the top three honors:

Opener	Responder
♠ A K 7 6 4 2	♠ Q 8
♡ J 3	♡ A 6
◇ 4	◇ A K Q J 8 7 6
♣ K J 5 4	♣ A 2
1♠	2◇
2♠	5NT
7♣	7◇
(pass)	

East locates two of the top three spade honors and signs off in seven diamonds, which makes thirteen tricks even when spades are 4-1.

SUPER-SCIENCE VARIATION

Sometimes the 5NT bidder is missing the jack or queen of his own strong suit, and is also missing the jack of opener's suit. For example, you might hold the same responding hand as above, without the queen or jack of diamonds:

♠ Q 8 ♡ A 6 5 ◇ A K Q 8 7 6 ♣ A 2

Partner	You
1♠	2◇
2♠	

You would like to play a grand slam in spades or diamonds, depending on which jack partner can produce. Can you ask partner to show the suit with the relevant jack? Here's a good but complicated method.

Responder to 5NT bids:

(a) *seven of his own suit = two of the top three honors plus the jack;*

(b) *seven of a lower suit = two of the top three honors without the jack, but a key queen in partner's bid suit, in case that is a useful filler;*

(c) *6NT = two of the top three honors without the jack and no outside key queen or jack;*

(d) one step above his trump suit at the six-level = two of the top three honors plus what looks like a key jack outside. (If spades are trumps, use 6♡ for this.) Over this, a relay asks where the key jack is.

Partner	You
2♡	3♢[1]
3♡	5NT
?	

1. Forcing.

Here's what partner's rebids would show:

    6♠ = two of the top three heart honors and the ♢J

    6NT = two of the top three honors without a key jack

    7♢ = two of the top three heart honors without the ♡J, but with the ♢Q

    7♡ = two of the top three heart honors with the ♡J

Suppose you, East, hold:

    ♠ A K Q 5 ♡ K 5 ♢ A K J 7 4 3 2 ♣ —

What would you bid in each case?

Partner	You
2♡	3♢
3♡	5NT
6NT	?

Bid 7♡ and hope for a 3-2 heart split.

Partner	You
2♡	3♢
3♡	5NT
7♢	?

Pass. If hearts break 4-1, the heart contracts will fail while you score up your grand slam in diamonds.

Partner	You
2♡	3♢
3♡	5NT
7♡	?

Pass. Obviously.

Unusual over Unusual – The Rest of the Story

8

PREVIEW

East-West are vulnerable. You, East, hold:

♠ 5 4 ♡ J 9 3 ◇ A Q 9 6 5 3 ♣ 10 9

West	North	East	South
			pass
1♣	2♣	?	

North's two-club bid was Michaels, showing at least 5-5 in the majors. What would you bid?

THE SOLUTION

The correct bid is two diamonds. This is a 'competitive' bid, and does not promise a strong hand. How can East show a strong hand?

    1. **Double.** This means, 'Partner, perhaps we can double them in something. I have one of the majors. If you have the other, they have no place to go.'

    2. **Two hearts.** Since North promised hearts and spades, this is a cuebid (see below for further explanation).

    3. **Two spades.** Again, this is a cuebid (see below for further explanation).

    This leaves the bids of 2◇ and 3♣ (and 3◇ for that matter) free to show competitive but not necessarily strong hands.

    The cuebids work this way: Cuebid the lower-ranking of their suits to show the lower-ranking of the other two suits, forcing. Cuebid the higher-ranking of their suits to show the higher-ranking of the other two suits, forcing. 'Forcing', in this context, means a limit raise or better. After a cuebid by responder, the opponents cannot play the hand undoubled. Either we play the hand or they play it doubled.

    For example:

Partner	Oppt	You	Oppt
1♦	2♦[1]	?	

1. Majors.

Here's what your bids mean now:

dbl	a penalty double of one major
2♡	clubs, forcing (limit raise strength or better)
2♠	diamond raise, forcing
2NT	natural, forcing
3♣	clubs, not forcing
3♦	diamonds, not forcing
3♡/3♠	splinters
3NT	16-17 natural, both majors stopped

This system applies over all specific two-suited bids by them. For example:

Partner	Oppt	You	Oppt
1♠	2♠[1]	?	

1. You are told this shows hearts and diamonds.

Your bids would mean the following:

dbl	I probably have a penalty double of either hearts or diamonds
2NT	natural, forcing
3♣	clubs, not forcing
3♦	cuebid of lower-ranking suit (i.e., limit raise strength or better with clubs)
3♡	cuebid of higher-ranking suit (i.e., a limit raise or better of spades)
3♠	competitive spade raise
3NT	natural, 16-17, both red suits stopped

Partner	Oppt	You	Oppt
1♡	2NT[1]	?	

1. Minors.

dbl	I probably have a penalty double of either diamonds or clubs
3♣	cuebid of lower-ranking suit (i.e., forcing heart raise)
3♦	cuebid of higher-ranking suit (i.e., forcing spade bid)
3♡	competitive heart raise
3♠	spade suit, not forcing
3NT	natural, 16-17, both minor suits stopped

The double may also be used on a hand where you don't actually have a penalty double, but where you have only one of RHO's suits stopped (so you can't bid 2NT or 3NT).

Back to the hand we started with:

E-W vulnerable

♠ 5 4   ♡ J 9 3   ◇ A Q 9 6 5 3   ♣ 10 9

West	North	East	South
			pass
1♣	2♣	?	

Despite the fact that East is vulnerable against not and has a flat distribution, it is not very risky to bid at the two-level. East has a six-card suit with two of the top three honors, and his partner opened vulnerable in second seat. This is East's one and only chance to compete.

The complete deal:

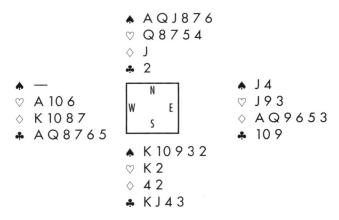

Here's what happened at the table:

West	North	East	South
			pass
1♣	2♣	pass	4♠
all pass			

The bidding should go:

West	North	East	South
			pass
1♣	2♣	2◇	4♠
5◇	5♠	pass	pass
?			

Now West is in the happy position of being unable to go minus. He can double 5♠ and take a plus, or he can press on to a speculative 6◇ which can actually be made on this layout!

This hand illustrates the extreme importance of being able to take advantage of the opponents' conventions to bid your own hands accurately. Notice that if North simply overcalls 1♠ instead of using Michaels, East is finished. South bids four spades, and West doesn't have enough to bid again.

Bread and Butter Conventions and Treatments

PART TWO

Help-Suit Game Tries

9

PREVIEW

You pick up, neither side vulnerable:

♠ K 6 3   ♡ A J 5 2   ◇ 6 4   ♣ 8 6 5 2

Partner opens 1♠. You raise to 2♠ and partner rebids 3♣. What is your call?

THE SOLUTION

The **Help-Suit Game Try** is a scientific device for bidding close games or staying out of bad ones. After opener's major-suit opening bid has been raised to the two-level, a new suit by opener is a game try, telling partner that if it's a close decision whether to bid game, to look at the 'help-suit' and see if he has any help there.

What is the definition of 'help there'? Responder imagines that opener has a weak four-card side suit and determines if he can cover some of those losers:

A singleton is helpful.
A doubleton is helpful if you have four trumps.
The ace is helpful, as is KQx(x).

Let's look at some examples:

♠ 8 6 5 2   ♡ A 7 6 5   ◇ 3 2   ♣ K 6 3

Partner	You
1♠	2♠
3♣/3◇/3♡	?

With the above hand, you accept a help-suit game try in any suit. (If partner bids 3♡, you raise to four, since there are times you will want to play the 4-4 fit instead of the 5-4.)

♠ J 6 5 2   ♡ 7 6   ◇ A K 3 2   ♣ 7 6 3

Partner	You
1♠	2♠
3♣/3◇/3♡	?

With the above hand, you accept only a help-suit game try in diamonds.

♠ 6 5 2   ♡ A 7 6 5   ◇ K Q 2   ♣ 7 6 3

Partner	You
1♠	2♠
3♣/3◇/3♡	?

With the above hand, you accept a game try in a red suit, but not in clubs (despite your maximum). Partner's hand for 3♣ will be something like:

♠ A K 8 4 3   ♡ K Q 4   ◇ A 5   ♣ 9 5 2

WHAT DO YOU LOSE BY PLAYING HELP-SUIT GAME TRIES?

You lose three things.

1. **You can't make a natural bid that might help you reach 3NT.** For example:

Opener	Responder
♠ A K 6 4 3	♠ J 5 2
♡ 8 7	♡ Q J 3 2
◇ K Q J 4	◇ 7 6 3
♣ A 2	♣ K Q 4

1♠	2♠
3◇	3NT
pass	

This would be a wonderful auction to the top contract, but using Help-Suit Game Tries, it can no longer be done, since 3◇ means something else.

2. **You lose the ability to make a natural slam try.**

Opener	Responder
♠ A Q 8 6 4 3	♠ K 5 2
♡ 8	♡ Q 6 3
◇ A K 8 4	◇ Q 7 6 3
♣ A 2	♣ Q J 4

Opener	Responder
1♠	2♠
3◇	?

Here opener wants to bid 3◇ as a natural slam try. Notice that they can make 6◇ on a 3-2 diamond break, while 6♠ makes only if the club finesse works. But playing Help-Suit Game Tries prevents this exploration.

3. The Help-Suit Game Try tells the opening leader too much about your hand.

Often it's right to lead the 'help suit' on opening lead, since declarer has identified it as his weak spot. This is especially true when the opponents stop in a partscore after using a help-suit game try. The good news is, however, that you can occasionally psyche a help-suit game try, if you want, and this may catch the opponents off guard. For example:

Opener	Responder
♠ A K 8 6 4 3	♠ Q 5 2
♡ K J 10 5 4	♡ 6 3 2
◇ A 8	◇ 7 6 3 2
♣ —	♣ A Q J

1♠	2♠
3♣	4♠

Here opener bids 3♣ to give the opponents the wrong picture of his hand. Maybe the opening lead will be a club, just what he wants!

Note: If you try this tactic more than once every few sessions, you'd better have your partner alert the opponents: 'Help-suit game try, usually, but my partner likes to fake this convention occasionally.'

Jacoby 2NT – New and Improved

The Jacoby 2NT convention, where 2NT in response to a major-suit opening bid shows a forcing raise of the major, is another of those things that have been adopted by many partnerships in some form. 'In some form' is the key phrase here; not everyone plays it the same way, and some ways are markedly better than others. For example, most people who play Jacoby 2NT play that a rebid of 4-of-the-major by opener is a minimum bid.

Opener	Responder
1♠	2NT[1]
4♠[2]	?

1. Jacoby
2. Minimum hand

The problem with this is that responder might want to make a slam try opposite even the most minimal of opening bids, and now he's forced to guess whether to bid past game in order to do so. For example, suppose responder has:

♠ Q 6 4 3   ♡ K J 7   ◇ A K 5 4   ♣ A 2

Most people would pass 4♠ without a second thought, but there are a number of minimums opener could hold that would make 6♠ either cold or odds-on:

Opener #1	Responder
♠ K J 8 5 2	♠ Q 6 4 3
♡ A 5 4	♡ K J 7
◇ Q 2	◇ A K 5 4
♣ K 6 3	♣ A 2

Opener #2	Responder
♠ A K 8 5 2	♠ Q 6 4 3
♡ Q 5 4	♡ K J 7
◇ 3 2	◇ A K 5 4
♣ K 6 3	♣ A 2

Opener #3	Responder
♠ A K 10 5 2	♠ Q 6 4 3
♡ A Q	♡ K J 7
◇ 6 3 2	◇ A K 5 4
♣ 7 4 3	♣ A 2

On the other hand, opposite the following minimums, you want to stay at the 4-level:

Opener #4	Responder
♠ A 8 7 5 2	♠ Q 6 4 3
♡ A Q 4	♡ K J 7
◇ 6 3 2	◇ A K 5 4
♣ K 4	♣ A 2

Opener #5	Responder
♠ K 8 7 5 2	♠ Q 6 4 3
♡ A 4	♡ K J 7
◇ J 3 2	◇ A K 5 4
♣ K Q 4	♣ A 2

Opener #6	Responder
♠ J 8 7 5 2	♠ Q 6 4 3
♡ A 3	♡ K J 7
◇ Q 3	◇ A K 5 4
♣ K Q J 4	♣ A 2

The main difference between the two sets of hands is the strength of the trump suit. When opener holds only one trump honor, responder, with Qxxx, Jxxx, 10xxx or xxxx, definitely does not want to go past game. However, if opener is going to jump to 4♠ with all minimums regardless of trump-suit quality, responder will often be endplayed into guessing what to do.

A better idea is for opener to rebid three spades with all minimums. Now 3NT by responder is an asking bid: 'What kind of minimum do you have?' With only one honor in trumps, opener signs off in game. With stronger trumps, opener can bid his side-suit strength.

So with hands #4, #5, and #6, the bidding goes:

Opener (#4, 5 or 6)	Responder
1♠	2NT
3♠[1]	3NT[2]
4♠[3]	

1. Minimum.
2. Asking.
3. Only one honor in trumps.

With the first two hands, the bidding goes:

Opener #1	Responder
♠ K J 8 5 2	♠ Q 6 4 3
♡ A 5 4	♡ K J 7
◇ Q 2	◇ A K 5 4
♣ K 6 3	♣ A 2

Opener #2	Responder
♠ A K 8 5 2	♠ Q 6 4 3
♡ Q 5 4	♡ K J 7
◇ 3 2	◇ A K 5 4
♣ K 6 3	♣ A 2

1♠	2NT
3♠[1]	3NT[2]
4♣[3]	

1. Minimum.
2. Asking.
3. More than one trump honor, plus an honor in clubs.

On hand #3, the auction would go like this:

Opener #3	Responder
♠ A K 10 5 2	♠ Q 6 4 3
♡ A Q	♡ K J 7
◇ 6 3 2	◇ A K 5 4
♣ 7 4 3	♣ A 2

1♠	2NT
3♠[1]	3NT[2]
4♡[3]	

1. Minimum.
2. Asking.
3. More than one trump honor, nothing in clubs or diamonds, but an honor (or two) in hearts.

If responder has good trumps himself and is looking for side-suit strength, he bids a new suit, asking about that suit:

Opener	Responder
♠ Q 7 6 4 2	♠ A K 8 3
♡ A K 6	♡ 8 5 4
◇ 3 2	◇ A Q J 5
♣ K 4 2	♣ A 5

1♠	2NT
3♠[1]	4♡[2]
5♡[3]	6♠

1. Minimum.
2. I have a slam try, but I'm weak here.
3. No problem.

Change opener's hand a little and you get:

Opener	Responder
♠ Q J 6 4 2	♠ A K 8 3
♡ Q J 6	♡ 8 5 4
◇ K 2	◇ A Q J 5
♣ K Q 2	♣ A 5

1♠	2NT
3♠[1]	4♡[2]
4♠[3]	pass

1. Minimum.
2. I have a slam try, but I'm weak here.
3. Sorry, can't help.

Since the opening leader in this actual deal had AKxxx of hearts, even 5♠ would have been too high (he played ace-king of hearts and gave partner a heart ruff).

ONE LAST POINT

If a 4♡ or 4♠ rebid no longer shows a minimum, you can use it as a 'trump cuebid.' This means: 'I have nothing to write home about, but I do have excellent trumps!'

Opener	Responder
♠ A K Q 6 4	♠ 8 5 3 2
♡ Q 7 2	♡ 4
◇ Q 6	◇ A K J 5
♣ 8 4 2	♣ A K J 3

1♠	2NT
4♠	6♠

Playing the old way, where a 4♠ rebid shows any minimum, responder is forced to guess whether to go or not.

Bread and Butter Conventions and Treatments

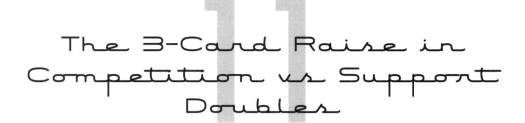

The 3-Card Raise in Competition vs Support Doubles

World Champion Eric Rodwell has made a number of contributions to bidding theory, but perhaps the most widely adopted of them is the **Support Double**. The Support Double, in case you're not familiar with it, works like this:

West	North	East	South
1◇	pass	1♠	2♣
?			

Now West has these options:

2♠	four-card spade support
dbl	three-card spade support
pass	fewer than three spades

This is very handy because when East holds only a four-card spade suit, he knows if he's on a seven-card fit as opposed to an eight-card fit and he can decide whether to compete further in his suit.

However, the price you pay is losing the penalty double. It has become popular to 'slip in' lead-directing bids, because players know they can't get penalized, but it's a shame to let them bid defensively with no risk. Even when an opponent has a good hand for his 'sandwich' overcall (an overcall between two bidders), there are chances for juicy penalties. . . if you can double. For example:

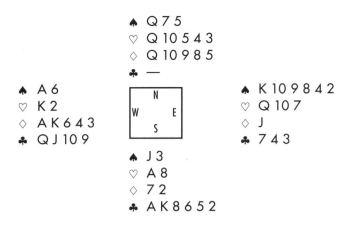

```
                    ♠ Q 7 5
                    ♡ Q 10 5 4 3
                    ◇ Q 10 9 8 5
                    ♣ —
    ♠ A 6                           ♠ K 10 9 8 4 2
    ♡ K 2              N            ♡ Q 10 7
    ◇ A K 6 4 3      W   E          ◇ J
    ♣ Q J 10 9         S            ♣ 7 4 3
                    ♠ J 3
                    ♡ A 8
                    ◇ 7 2
                    ♣ A K 8 6 5 2
```

West	North	East	South
1◇	pass	1♠	2♣
?			

Using Support Doubles, West must pass, and East will rebid 2♠. Without Support Doubles, West doubles two clubs and collects 500 or 800.

Another advantage of raising with three trumps rather than making a Support Double is that your raise takes up their valuable bidding space. For example:

Both vul.

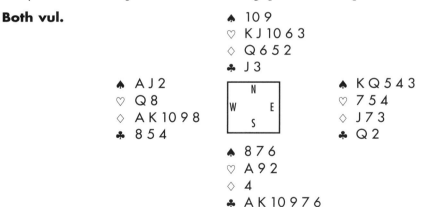

```
                    ♠ 10 9
                    ♡ K J 10 6 3
                    ◇ Q 6 5 2
                    ♣ J 3
    ♠ A J 2                          ♠ K Q 5 4 3
    ♡ Q 8              N             ♡ 7 5 4
    ◇ A K 10 9 8     W   E           ◇ J 7 3
    ♣ 8 5 4            S             ♣ Q 2
                    ♠ 8 7 6
                    ♡ A 9 2
                    ◇ 4
                    ♣ A K 10 9 7 6
```

Compare the Support Double auction:

West	North	East	South
1◇	pass	1♠	2♣
dbl	2♡	2♠	4♡
all pass			

resulting in North-South +620, with the natural raise auction:

West	North	East	South
1♦	pass	1♠	2♣
2♠	all pass		

resulting in North-South −110.

Finally and ironically, sometimes the Support Double takes up your own bidding space:

Both vul.

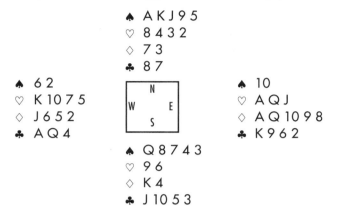

West	North	East	South
		1♦	pass
1♡	1♠	dbl[1]	3♠
all pass			

1. Support Double.

East-West result: +100. Whose fault is this one, East's or West's? We don't know, but their auction was certainly problematic. Here they are, on a finesse for 6♦, settling for +100 defending 3♠.

Without the Support Double, the auction goes:

West	North	East	South
		1♦	pass
1♡	1♠	2♣	3♠
4♦	pass	4♡	pass
5♦	all pass		

and East-West score +600.

The Support Double showed:

- three hearts
- a hand of any strength

The natural two-club bid showed:

- five diamonds
- four or more clubs
- a good hand (for the vulnerable free-bid)

Clearly, much more information was conveyed with the natural bid.

One last thing to consider on the Support Double side — suppose West had five hearts and three diamonds:

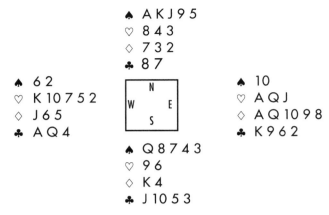

♠ A K J 9 5
♡ 8 4 3
◇ 7 3 2
♣ 8 7

♠ 6 2
♡ K 10 7 5 2
◇ J 6 5
♣ A Q 4

♠ 10
♡ A Q J
◇ A Q 10 9 8
♣ K 9 6 2

♠ Q 8 7 4 3
♡ 9 6
◇ K 4
♣ J 10 5 3

West	North	East	South
		1◇	pass
1♡	1♠	2♣	3♠
?			

Notice that nothing has been lost. West still has enough to bid four diamonds freely, and this time he'll pass East's four-heart bid. If South bids four spades instead of three, it's true that East-West will lose their eight-card heart fit (West will bid 5◇), but that's a loss of only 50 points (+600 instead of +650).

Bread and Butter Conventions and Treatments

56 | The 3-Card Raise vs. Support Doubles

Four-card Majors in Third and Fourth Seat

Agreeing to open four-card majors is not really a convention, and indeed, it was once the norm. Today, however, it is unusual, although many experts play four-card majors frequently, including Bob Hamman, Eddie Kantar, and Paul Soloway, among others. However, even five-card major players often open with four-baggers opposite a passed partner to avoid this kind of bidding accident:

Partner	**You**
♠ A K 7 5 3	♠ 6 4 2
♡ Q 8 7 3 2	♡ A K 5 4
◇ 3 2	◇ 6 5
♣ 7	♣ A 8 4 3

Partner	**Oppt**	**You**	**Oppt**
pass	pass	1♣	pass
1♠	all pass		

Playing four-card majors, you open 1♡ instead and your partner forces to game. Without four-card majors, you are forced to bid again as a third-seat opener with the above hand in case there's a heart fit; now partner will think you have a full opening bid and you will often get too high:

Partner	You
♠ A 8 7 5 3	♠ 6 4 2
♡ Q 2	♡ A K 5 4
◇ Q 2	◇ 6 5
♣ K 7 5 2	♣ A 8 4 3

Partner	Oppt	You	Oppt
pass	pass	1♣	pass
1♠	pass	1NT	pass
3♣	all pass		

This auction shows what happens if you open light in a minor suit and take another bid -- you get overboard. Had you opened with 1♡, the bidding would have gone

Partner	Oppt	You	Oppt
pass	pass	1♡	pass
1♠	pass	pass	

If the opponents want to push you up to the two-level, that's fine; and if the opponents push themselves up to the three-level, you can double them.

The idea of the light third-seat four-card major is that you plan to make only one bid, but if you hit partner with a big distributional fit, you can also reach game. The four-card majors opposite a passed hand rule is:

> *If you are going to open the bidding in third or fourth seat with a light*
> *hand, and you are not going to take a second bid voluntarily, open with*
> *your four-card major.*

The benefit of this agreement is that you can still reach game when it's there, which, after all, is the biggest bonus for opening the bidding. A further benefit is that your major-suit opening bid makes it more difficult for the opponents to get into the bidding. For example, after you open 1♣, they can bid anything they like at the one-level, but after you open 1♠, they have to bid at the two-level, which requires a stronger hand or involves taking more risk.

If you play modified Drury (page 30), you can show partner whether you opened on a four-card or five-card suit, and he can show you if he's got three- or four-card support. By the way, the four-card major opening also works perfectly with forcing notrump responses, because you simply pass the forcing notrump.

A USEFUL ADJUNCT

Suppose you have 1-5-4-3 shape and a light hand. You open 1♡ in third or fourth seat and partner responds with 1♠. What are you going to do? If you bid again, your partner will think you have a full opening bid and you'll get too high. On the other hand, you can hardly pass and leave partner in a possible four-one fit. The answer is: open with two hearts in third seat!

Bread and Butter Conventions and Treatments

Here are two example deals from OKbridge.

Both vul.

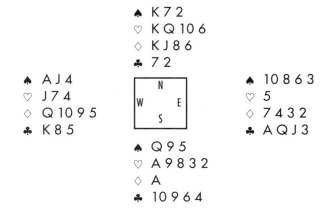

```
                    ♠ K 7 2
                    ♡ K Q 10 6
                    ◇ K J 8 6
                    ♣ 7 2
    ♠ A J 4              N              ♠ 10 8 6 3
    ♡ J 7 4         W         E         ♡ 5
    ◇ Q 10 9 5           S              ◇ 7 4 3 2
    ♣ K 8 5                             ♣ A Q J 3
                    ♠ Q 9 5
                    ♡ A 9 8 3 2
                    ◇ A
                    ♣ 10 9 6 4
```

West	North	East	South
		pass	pass
pass	1♡	pass	4◇[1]
pass	4♡	all pass	

1. Splinter.

North-South reached game because North opened a four-card major in fourth seat. In this case, North can pass a one-spade response. Had North opened one diamond and South bid one heart, North would have had the unhappy choice of taking a second bid with a minimum, or failing to raise with excellent support, thereby possibly missing a game. Since the money is in the majors and not the minors, North can get the hand off his chest with a one-heart opening bid and then call it a day.

Is 4♡ a good game? If hearts are 2-2, it's cold. If not, there are many chances: a friendly spade situation or opening lead (East actually led the ♠6, picking up the suit for declarer), the ◇Q falling third, the opponents being unable to play trumps three times, or, if all else fails, a misdefense.

Both vul.

<pre>
                          ♠ A 8 6 5 4
                          ♡ A 9 8 7 5
                          ◇ 10 6 3
                          ♣ —
        ♠ 10 7   ┌─────────┐   ♠ 3 2
        ♡ K Q J 3   │   N   │   ♡ 10 6 4
        ◇ J 8 5   │ W   E │   ◇ K Q 7 4
        ♣ K J 9 2   │   S   │   ♣ A Q 5 3
                        └─────────┘
                          ♠ K Q J 9
                          ♡ 2
                          ◇ A 9 2
                          ♣ 10 8 7 6 4
</pre>

West	North	East	South
pass	pass	pass	1♠
pass	4♣[1]	pass	4♠
all pass			

1. Splinter.

This time, the four-card major bid created a game swing out of thin air.

Ogust Responses to Weak Twos

After a weak two-bid in a major and a 2NT response, opener uses step responses to show various types of hands for his weak two-bid. The original **Ogust** convention worked like this:

Opener	Responder
2♡ or 2♠	2NT
?	
3♣	bad hand, bad suit
3♢	bad hand, good suit
3♡	good hand, bad suit
3♠	good hand, good suit
3NT	AKQxxx

The general rule was simple: 'bad hands first'.

There was one flaw. When opener started with 2♠ and rebid 3♡, there was no room for responder to show a heart suit, an alternative place to play when opener's spade suit was bad. So many partnerships switched 3♢ and 3♡ to read this way:

3♣	bad suit, bad hand
3♢	bad suit, good hand
3♡	good suit, bad hand
3♠	good suit, good hand
3NT	AKQxxx

So the new rule was 'bad suits first'.

For example:

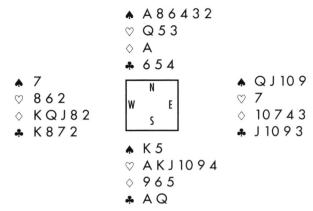

```
             ♠ A 8 6 4 3 2
             ♡ Q 5 3
             ◇ A
             ♣ 6 5 4
♠ 7                              ♠ Q J 10 9
♡ 8 6 2          N               ♡ 7
◇ K Q J 8 2    W   E             ◇ 10 7 4 3
♣ K 8 7 2        S               ♣ J 10 9 3
             ♠ K 5
             ♡ A K J 10 9 4
             ◇ 9 6 5
             ♣ A Q
```

West	North	East	South
	2♠	pass	2NT
pass	3◇[1]	pass	3♡
pass	4◇[2]	pass	6♡
all pass			

1. Bad suit, good hand.
2. Cuebid in support of hearts.

Notice that four spades makes four, and six hearts makes six!

Using 3◇ to show the good hand, bad suit, allows responder to show his heart suit on the way to 3NT or 4♠. In this case, opener is so delighted, he can cuebid with his fine controls.

Note: After a 2◇ weak two-bid, Ogust doesn't apply, although some partnerships use a 3♣ rebid as a good hand and 3◇ as a bad hand.

There are many other forms of Ogust methods that have cropped up over the years, some that include the ability to show a five-card weak two-bid or a singleton. Here's a method that caters to opening a weak two-bid with a side four-card major:

Opener	Responder
2♡/2♠	2NT
?	
3♣	bad suit (with a bad hand or a good hand)
3◇	good hand, good suit (game force)
3 of the opening major	bad hand, good suit
3 of the other major	natural, 4-card major
3NT	AKQxxx

Over the 3♣ rebid, responder bids 3◇ as a strong game try, while three of opener's major is invitational but weaker. Three of the new major by responder is natural and forcing.

Over 3◇, responder bids three of a new major as natural and forcing, while three of the original major is also forcing, asking for a cuebid.

WHAT DO YOU LOSE BY PLAYING OGUST?

By playing Ogust responses to 2NT, you give up the natural or feature-showing rebids, which may point the way to the best game contract. For example, playing 'feature', responder bids 2NT with this hand:

♠ A 4   ♡ K 5 2   ◇ A Q 9 7 5 4   ♣ K 3

After a 2♠ opening bid, he hears 3◇! So he bids 3NT instead of 4♠. Partner holds:

♠ K Q 8 7 6 3   ♡ 9 8 4   ◇ K J 2   ♣ 6

3NT is a superior contract to 4♠, which may go down when spades break 4-1 or if the heart ace is offside.

Clarifying Cuebids

Clarifying Cuebids is a fancy name for a simple principle in a common auction: when opener jump rebids his suit, all bids below 3NT are an attempt to reach 3NT from the right side. First, here's an Okbridge example of why this kind of agreement is useful:

Both vul.

```
                    ♠ A Q 7
                    ♡ J 10 8 4 2
                    ◇ 8
                    ♣ J 9 7 6
      ♠ K 8                          ♠ J 9 6 4
      ♡ A K Q 9 7 5     N            ♡ 3
      ◇ J 9          W     E         ◇ A K Q 7 5 3
      ♣ A 5 2           S            ♣ 8 3
                    ♠ 10 5 3 2
                    ♡ 6
                    ◇ 10 6 4 2
                    ♣ K Q 10 4
```

West	North	East	South
			pass
1♡	pass	2◇	pass
3♡	pass	3NT	all pass

East came out smelling like a rose when dummy hit with a club stopper and ten tricks were readily available. This was a big pickup because many pairs played in 4♡, down three. Why did East bid 3NT with no club stopper? Because he was endplayed into bidding 3NT by his 2/1 system, in which a jump rebid of opener's suit over an initial 2/1 response requires responder to cuebid. With no black-suit cuebid available, East decided to make the practical but risky bid of three notrump and hope for the best. But suppose the hands had been:

West	East
♠ A K 8	♠ J 9 6 4
♡ A K Q 9 7 5	♡ 3
◇ J 9	◇ A K Q 7 5 3
♣ 5 2	♣ 8 3

Now East-West belong in 5◇, not 3NT, but the bidding would have gone the same way.

Playing that all bids below 3NT are an attempt to reach 3NT, the bidding goes (on the real-life hand):

West	East
♠ K 8	♠ J 9 6 4
♡ A K Q 9 7 5	♡ 3
◇ J 9	◇ A K Q 7 5 3
♣ A 5 2	♣ 8 3

West	East
1♡	2◇
3♡	3♠[1]
3NT	

1. Spade stopper.

On the hand revised as we showed it above:

West	East
♠ A K 8	♠ J 9 6 4
♡ A K Q 9 7 5	♡ 3
◇ J 9	◇ A K Q 7 5 3
♣ 5 2	♣ 8 3

West	East
1♡	2◇
3♡	3♠[1]
4◇[2]	5◇

1. Spade stopper.
2. Having already described a very strong six-card heart suit, opener now shows secondary diamond support and leaves it to his partner to place the contract.

WHAT IF YOU WANT TO CUEBID?

In the words of the commercial, just do it! You can clarify your bid later:

Partner	You
1♡	2◇
3♡	3♠
3NT	4♡

If your spade bid showed a stopper, you would pass 3NT. When you bid 4♡, it becomes obvious that your 3♠ bid was a cuebid. The hands might be:

Partner	You
♠ J 4	♠ A 3
♡ A K Q 9 8 2	♡ 10 5 3
◇ 7 2	◇ A K Q J 10
♣ A K 3	♣ 7 6 2

The bidding continues:

1♡	2◇
3♡	3♠
3NT	4♡
4NT	5♡
5NT	7NT

Another example:

Opener	Responder
♠ K Q 2	♠ A 3
♡ A K Q J 8 2	♡ 10 5 3
◇ 2	◇ A K Q J 10
♣ Q J 10	♣ 7 6 2

1♡	2◇
3♡	3♠
3NT	4♡
pass	

Opener reluctantly passes 4♡ because with both spade and club controls, responder bids 4♣ over 3NT (another cuebid). Here's that auction in practice:

Opener	Responder
♠ K Q 2	♠ A 3
♡ A K Q J 8 2	♡ 10 5 3
◇ 2	◇ A Q J 10 9
♣ Q J 10	♣ K 6 2

1♡	2◇
3♡	3♠
3NT	4♣
4NT	5♡
6♡	pass

The Natural (Forcing) 2NT Response to a 1♣ or 1◇ Opening Bid

One of the fascinating things about bridge is that bidding systems develop over the years just as a language does. For example, the meaning of this fairly common auction has changed quite a lot:

Opener	Responder
1♣/1◇	2NT

It was once Standard to play this sequence as forcing, but now that's practically a 'convention', because a 2NT response to one-of-a-minor is generally used to describe an 11-12 point balanced hand.

Playing the 2NT bid as invitational caters to light opening bids. However, while most players will stretch and open light with a five-card major, or with a balanced hand with four hearts, many will pass an 11- or 12-point hand without either a five-card major or hearts. Therefore, the non-forcing 2NT response is unnecessary over a minor-suit opening.

Additionally, there is a problem with all limit-bid responses: how can you know when game makes? Some 12-opposite-12 or 13-opposite-11 games roll home, and some 28-point games fail. Why design a constructive bidding system to cater to playing a hand in exactly 2NT and taking exactly eight tricks? Also, if 2NT is invitational, responder must bid 3NT with a balanced 13+ count and that preempts his own auction. And finally, there is nothing easier than playing against a declarer who, by passing the 2NT response, shows exactly 11 or 12 points — you can count every point and place partner's high cards!

A BETTER 2NT CONVENTION

If you beef up the opening one-of-a-minor bid just a little, you can dump 2NT not forcing. Even with a good 11 points, you can respond 2NT and most of the time your partner will have 13 points and you'll have at least 24 points for your 3NT game.

Example: You open 1◇ with this 12 count:

♠ Q 5 2   ♡ K 3   ◇ A 9 6 5 4   ♣ K 10 3

and partner bids 2NT, invitational. You, of course, pass. Suppose partner held:

a)   ♠ K J 6   ♡ Q J 5   ◇ K J 3   ♣ 9 6 5 2

b)   ♠ A J 10   ♡ A 5 2   ◇ 7 3   ♣ Q 9 6 5 2

c)   ♠ J 6 4   ♡ A 5   ◇ 8 7 3 2   ♣ A Q 4 2

d)   ♠ A J 6   ♡ A J 5   ◇ 3 2   ♣ J 9 6 5 2

You can see that 3NT has a reasonable play opposite any of these 11-counts, but you will be in 2NT. In addition, when 3NT fails, 2NT will often fail as well.

These examples total only 23 points between the two hands, but you'll play in 2NT with 24 and even 25 total points sometimes (when opener doesn't like his 13-count), and miss game. And remember, a good principle of bridge is to bid plenty of games and keep the opponents under pressure. Sometimes the opponents get off to the wrong lead, or sometimes the cards lie well for you. Your risk is a partscore swing when there are exactly eight tricks (if there are fewer, 2NT was going down anyway), and your gain can be huge, especially when vulnerable at IMPs.

The 2NT forcing response is also a great space-saver. Suppose you open 1◇ and partner responds 2NT. You hold one of the following:

a)   ♠ 5   ♡ A 3   ◇ A K 8 7 5 4   ♣ K 4 3 2

b)   ♠ Q 5   ♡ 3   ◇ A K 7 5 4   ♣ A 10 9 4 2

c)   ♠ Q 5   ♡ A 3   ◇ K Q J 5 4   ♣ K 4 3 2

d)   ♠ 5 4   ♡ 3   ◇ A K J 7 5 4   ♣ A 4 3 2

You can rebid 3♣, forcing, on any of these hands; now you still have room to explore for a possible slam below 3NT. Partner's hand was actually:

♠ A K J   ♡ Q J   ◇ 9 6 3 2   ♣ Q J 6 5

If partner responds 3NT to your 1◇ opening (because 2NT is not forcing) on this hand, you must pass with all four of our example hands, and not once are you in the right spot!

Suppose you open a minor and partner bids 2NT, forcing. Partner denies a four-card major, so what does it mean if you rebid a major? For example:

You	Partner
1◇	2NT
3♡	

You can play that it shows shortness; or you can play that it's a five-card suit and you are 6-5; or you can play that you have a good stopper here and are worried about the other major. Take your pick and make an agreement with your partner.

If 2NT is forcing, you can use the direct jump to 3NT to show a mild slam invitation, showing a 16-18 notrump. If opener now wants to show a second suit, he can do so safely at the four-level, and not be worried about getting too high. A 4NT rebid by responder in this auction, by the way, is natural, showing no interest in opener's suit(s):

Example #1

You	Partner
1◇	3NT[1]
4♣	4NT[2]

1. 16-18 balanced.
2. No interest in either minor.

Example #2

You	Partner
♠ Q J 5	♠ A K 6
♡ 3	♡ A 5 4
◇ K J 8 6 2	◇ Q 5 3
♣ A K 9 4	♣ Q J 8 7

1◇	3NT[1]
4♣	4♠[2]
5♠[3]	6♣
pass	

1. 16-18 balanced.
2. Concentration of strength; probably not so good in other major.
3. Shape-showing bid which he makes because he now knows notrump is the wrong place to play.

There was no diamond ruff, so you play in 6♣ making six, while the rest of the field plays in 3NT down one (after 1◇-3NT).

Jordan 2NT

PREVIEW

You pick up:

♠ A 4 2   ♡ 5 3   ◇ K Q 6 5 2   ♣ J 10 7

Partner opens 1◇. The next hand doubles. What is your call?

THE SOLUTION

Using the Jordan convention, a jump to 2NT over a takeout double shows a limit raise in partner's suit.

This allows you to use the jump to the three-level in partner's suit as preemptive. It also provides room for partner to make a game try at the three-level or slam try at the four-level (a jump can be used to show shortness).

West	East
♠ A K 7 6 5 3	♠ Q J 4 2
♡ K Q 5	♡ A 6 3
◇ 6	◇ 7 4 3 2
♣ A 7 2	♣ K 5

West	North	East	South
1♠	dbl	2NT	pass
4◇			

Over 4◇, this responder should go to slam. He has all working values.

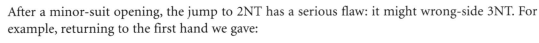

After a minor-suit opening, the jump to 2NT has a serious flaw: it might wrong-side 3NT. For example, returning to the first hand we gave:

♠ A 4 2   ♡ 5 3   ◇ K Q 6 5 2   ♣ J 10 7

Partner opens 1◇. The next hand doubles.

If 3NT becomes the final contract, which often happens after a minor-suit fit is established, the opening bidder should declare the hand because he might hold something like:

♠ Q J 5   ♡ K 4   ◇ A J 7 4 3   ♣ A K 6

3NT is a great spot, but only if the opening lead is coming up to this hand. If responder declares, a heart lead will probably defeat the contract.

Some people reverse the meaning of 2NT and the jump raise after a minor-suit opening is doubled. They would therefore play this sequence to show a limit raise:

Opener	Oppt	Responder	Oppt
1◇	dbl	3◇	

while this one

Opener	Oppt	Responder	Oppt
1◇	dbl	2NT	

is a preemptive raise in diamonds.

This is nice, up to a point. But one day you might make a preemptive raise, and partner, with a giant hand, wants to play 3NT. Again, the contract will be played by the wrong hand!

Opener	Responder
♠ A Q J	♠ 5 2
♡ K 6 4	♡ 8 7 3
◇ K 6 5 3	◇ A Q 10 7 2
♣ A Q 7	♣ 6 4 3

Opener	Oppt	Responder	Oppt
1◇	dbl	2NT	

So using 2NT as the preemptive raise may also backfire!

There are other variations, such as using a jump to the other minor as a limit raise; this keeps 2NT free for some other meaning. In this method, both these sequences show a limit raise:

Opener	Oppt	Responder	Oppt
1♦	dbl	3♣	

Opener	Oppt	Responder	Oppt
1♣	dbl	2♦	

This is preferable, although it does use up the 3♣ and 2♦ bids, which might otherwise be played as natural or fit-showing. In the end, no matter which toy you choose, you'll have to give up something.

New Suits Not Forcing in Competition

Some of the most important and basic agreements for any partnership revolve around which sequences are forcing and which are not. The issues involved will have a great impact on the range of actions available to the partnership, especially in competitive situations. Look at this example. You, South, hold:

Both vul.

♠ K J 7 3 2   ♡ 9   ◇ 10 8 3 2   ♣ 7 4 2

West	North	East	South
	1♡	dbl	?

Do you want to bid 1♠ now? Does your system allow you to?

At one table in a Swiss Teams match, North-South played that a new suit was forcing in this situation, just as though the double had not occurred. At the other table, North-South played that a new suit was not forcing. Here's what happened:

Table One

West	North	East	South
1♡	dbl	pass	pass
pass			

Table Two

West	North	East	South
1♡	dbl	1♠	pass
4◇¹	pass	4♠	all pass

1. Splinter

The whole deal:

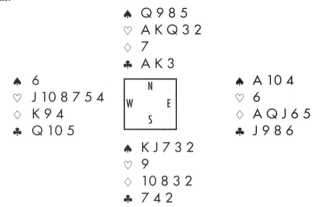

```
                    ♠ Q 9 8 5
                    ♡ A K Q 3 2
                    ♢ 7
                    ♣ A K 3
  ♠ 6                                    ♠ A 10 4
  ♡ J 10 8 7 5 4          N              ♡ 6
  ♢ K 9 4           W         E          ♢ A Q J 6 5
  ♣ Q 10 5                S              ♣ J 9 8 6
                    ♠ K J 7 3 2
                    ♡ 9
                    ♢ 10 8 3 2
                    ♣ 7 4 2
```

At Table Two, South made ten tricks in four spades for +620.

At the other table, North was very pleased to play in one heart doubled. . . until he saw the dummy. He ended up taking one spade, four hearts and two clubs, making seven tricks, for +160. For some strange reason, it is popular to play new suits forcing over takeout doubles and after overcalls. A similar scenario to the one that took place above could have occurred after an overcall by partner. Suppose the bidding goes:

Oppt	Partner	Oppt	You
1♣	1♡	pass	?

Why should you be forced to pass with the KQ10xx in spades and out? You might have a game or partscore in spades, or need the spade lead to defeat their 3NT game. Suppose you have this hand, which is similar to the South hand above, only with better spades.

♠ K Q 10 5 3 ♡ 9 ♢ 10 8 3 2 ♣ 7 4 2

If your system allows you to bid 1♠, you gain when partner has any of the following hands:

(a)   ♠ A 8 4 2 ♡ Q 10 6 5 3 ♢ 4 ♣ A Q J

(b)   ♠ 2 ♡ A K 6 5 2 ♢ A K 5 4 ♣ 8 5 3

(c)   ♠ J 2 ♡ K Q 6 5 3 ♢ A 6 5 4 ♣ Q 3

With hand (a), partner bids game and you score up +620 (probably). With hand (b), partner bids 2♢, you pass, and you play in the superior partscore. With hand (c), they play the hand, probably in notrump, and partner gets off to the ♠J lead instead of the costly heart lead.

The new-suit-forcing idea after an overcall became popular to simplify this sequence:

Oppt	Partner	Oppt	You
1◇	1♡	pass	2◇

For simplicity, people like to play that the cuebid promises a fit for partner's overcall. If a new suit is not forcing, then the cuebid becomes 'confusing' since it does not necessarily show a fit (i.e., you might be preparing to make a forcing bid in another suit). It's true that cuebid-promises-a-fit makes life easy sometimes, but we think the price you pay is too high. People who play this way often find themselves in extremely uncomfortable situations.

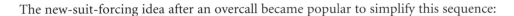

PAMELA'S TALE OF WOE

Matchpoints
Both vul.
You hold:

♠ 10 4   ♡ 7   ◇ J 10 3 2   ♣ A Q J 9 3 2

Partner	Oppt	You	Oppt
1♡	dbl	?	

A hand like this came up in the final of a National Pairs Event. I (Pamela) was forced to pass, because we played that a new suit was forcing. I felt very uncomfortable about this because for one thing, it might be our hand for three notrump if my clubs come in for six tricks, and for another, my partner might need to find a club lead against their contract to set it. An alternative to passing was 3♣, a weak jump shift (see page 25), except that partner would expect a weaker hand and I didn't want to miss 3NT. So I passed, planning to show my suit on the next round.

Here's what happened next:

Partner	Oppt	You	Oppt
1♡	dbl	pass	2♠
pass	pass	?	

I now bid three clubs and got doubled. The whole deal was:

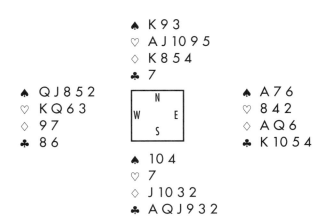

                    ♠ K 9 3
                    ♡ A J 10 9 5
                    ◇ K 8 5 4
                    ♣ 7

♠ Q J 8 5 2   ┌─────────┐   ♠ A 7 6
♡ K Q 6 3   │   N   │   ♡ 8 4 2
◇ 9 7   │ W   E │   ◇ A Q 6
♣ 8 6   │   S   │   ♣ K 10 5 4
                    └─────────┘

                    ♠ 10 4
                    ♡ 7
                    ◇ J 10 3 2
                    ♣ A Q J 9 3 2

They took two spades, two diamonds and a diamond ruff, and one club (I finessed the nine). We went −500 for a zero. My partner was very nice about it, but I vowed never to play this silly system again. Suppose I had been allowed to bid 2♣, not forcing:

Partner	Oppt	You	Oppt
1♡	dbl	2♣	2♠
all pass			

Having bid my hand already, I feel no obligation to balance over 2♠. Partner leads her singleton club. I win and play a heart through. She wins and returns a heart. I ruff and play ace and a club. She ruffs (or overruffs) and gives me a second heart ruff. We score +100. Now it's true that I could have passed out two spades on the auction we had, and we could have defeated it one trick, but how was I supposed to know? What if the hands had been like this:

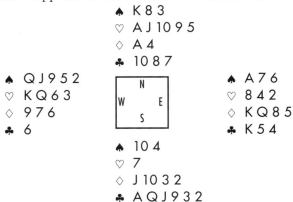

                    ♠ K 8 3
                    ♡ A J 10 9 5
                    ◇ A 4
                    ♣ 10 8 7

♠ Q J 9 5 2   ┌─────────┐   ♠ A 7 6
♡ K Q 6 3   │   N   │   ♡ 8 4 2
◇ 9 7 6   │ W   E │   ◇ K Q 8 5
♣ 6   │   S   │   ♣ K 5 4
                    └─────────┘

                    ♠ 10 4
                    ♡ 7
                    ◇ J 10 3 2
                    ♣ A Q J 9 3 2

Again, I pass out 2♠. Partner finds the club lead. I win and return a heart. She wins and returns the jack of hearts; I ruff, and return a diamond. She wins and gives me a second heart ruff. They take a spade finesse and claim. Meanwhile, I can make 3♣ even if they play trumps, because when I try to negotiate my diamond ruff, by playing a diamond to the ace and a diamond, East will win an honor. I can pick up the trumps, losing two spades and two diamonds.

If we're playing hardball, we might even get to 3NT from the North side and make it. If East leads a spade, partner finesses in clubs for nine tricks. If East leads a diamond (high or low), it's the same thing (the second diamond trick provides trick number nine). If East leads a heart (unlikely), North wins and knocks out the other high heart. Since spades are blocked, he again takes a club finesse for the contract. Very nice; 3NT cold and I'm -110 against two spades.

The lesson here is to redouble with ten points or more (old-fashioned but sensible), and to play that new suits are not forcing. (By the way, when I have redoubled with a five-card suit and ten-plus points, they have ended up playing in my five-card suit — doubled — more than once.)

AFTERTHOUGHT

After an overcall, what do we do about the confusing cuebid if we're going to play that new suits are not forcing?

When you have support for partner's suit, you may wish to raise directly instead of cuebidding. When your partner overcalls with a suit, it's not necessary to cuebid every single time you have ten points and support. It's not against the law with ten points and three trumps to raise to the two-level (you're allowed to have maximum dummies sometimes). The opponents often give you a chance to show that your raise was maximum. And with four trumps and a fair hand, raise to game! Why pussyfoot around with a dainty cuebid? Put the pressure on 'em! If you have four trumps, it's unlikely that anything horrible will happen (unless partner really stepped out this time...).

Slow Arrival

You pick up:

♠ 4   ♡ J 8 5 4 2   ◇ A K Q 6 3   ♣ A 4

	Partner	You
	1♠	2♡
	4♡	?

What is your call?

THE SOLUTION

Of course, the answer depends on what partner's 4♡ bid means. **Fast Arrival** means that the jump to game, when a lower bid in the same suit would have been forcing, is weak. For example, in this sequence:

	Partner	You
	1◇	2♡[1]
	4♡	?

1. Strong.

After a strong jump shift, a raise is forcing, so what is the meaning of the jump to game? Playing Fast Arrival, the jump shows a minimum hand. This is a popular method for partnerships playing a strong club system. Usually one hand knows that partner is limited and can see no chance for slam, so he jumps to game as a sign-off. In Standard bidding, Fast Arrival doesn't work so well. In fact, even in strong club sequences, Fast Arrival may backfire. But there is an alternative method: **Slow Arrival**.

Slow Arrival is more complicated, but more accurate. With this agreement, the jump to game when a lower bid in the same suit would have been forcing shows either strong trumps or a hand with nice controls for slam and decent trumps. ('Decent' trumps include a top honor.) The simple raise shows a minimum hand or a hand that wants to set the trump suit and is planning to go past game regardless of partner's next bid.

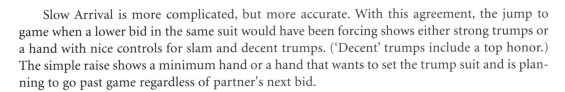

A WORD OF WARNING

Fast Arrival and Slow Arrival do not apply when the lower bid in the same suit would not have been forcing. For example:

Opener	Responder
1♣	1♠
4♠	

This has nothing to do with Fast Arrival or Slow Arrival, because 3♠ is not forcing.

Opener	Responder
1♡	2♡
4♡	

Again, this auction is not relevant. Since 3♡ is not forcing, 4♡ has no particular meaning beyond a desire to play game.

Opener	Responder
1♠	1NT
2♡	4♡

3♡ is not forcing, so, again, 4♡ has no meaning beyond a desire to play game.

Partner	You
1♠	2♡
4♡	?

Here is the auction we started with. It qualifies as an example of Fast Arrival or Slow Arrival, assuming you play the raise to 3♡ as forcing. If 3♡ is forcing, the jump to 4♡ describes a certain type of hand, depending on whether you adopt Fast Arrival or Slow Arrival as your partnership style.

Let's say you pick up a great hand. Would you rather be playing Fast Arrival or Slow Arrival? Here's the scenario. You hold:

♠ K 6 5 3   ♡ —   ◇ A K Q 5 4 3   ♣ A K 4

You	Partner
1◇	1♡
2♠	4♠[1]

1. Fast Arrival.

You want to be in slam if your partner holds good trumps, but if your partner holds poor trumps, you'd certainly prefer to stop in game. Playing Fast Arrival, you have the above sequence. What would you do? Whatever you do, you are completely guessing. You already knew partner was weak since you have the rest of the deck, so what good was Fast Arrival?

Suppose you are instead playing Slow Arrival. Slow Arrival uses an unnecessary jump to show specifically good trumps or a slam try with nice controls and decent trumps.

Good trumps are defined as:

a) **two of the top three honors; or**

b) **one top honor with extra length; or**

c) **great trumps in context of the auction.** For example, if your partner shows a strong-two bid in spades, and you have Jxxx of spades, this is a great trump holding.

Here's your great hand again:

$$\spadesuit \ K\,6\,5\,3 \quad \heartsuit \ — \quad \diamondsuit \ A\,K\,Q\,5\,4\,3 \quad \clubsuit \ A\,K\,4$$

Playing Slow Arrival, you could have one of these auctions:

You	Partner
1♦	1♡
2♠	3♠

Partner's 3♠ is simply a forcing raise; no further information is available at this point.

You	Partner
1♦	1♡
2♠	4♠

The 4♠ bid is limited but shows good trumps or good controls for slam; in this case it must be good trumps, since you have most of the controls.

On the first auction, you know your partner does not have good trumps (unless he's going to slam by himself, in which case, you're not involved). You will try for slam anyway by bidding at the four level (4♣) to see if your partner can 'squeak'.

$$\spadesuit \ K\,6\,5\,3 \quad \heartsuit \ — \quad \diamondsuit \ A\,K\,Q\,5\,4\,3 \quad \clubsuit \ A\,K\,4$$

You	Partner
1♦	1♡
2♠	3♠
4♣	?

If your partner bids 4♠, you'll give up. But partner might have something like:

$$\spadesuit \ A\,8\,4\,2 \quad \heartsuit \ Q\,9\,7\,5\,3 \quad \diamondsuit \ J\,6 \quad \clubsuit \ 7\,3$$

Having bid three spades, denying great trumps, your partner should squeak over your 4♣ bid (by bidding 4◇), and this is all you need to hear for slam.

Squeak Bids (known also as *Squeeze Bids* or *Last Train to Clarkesville* bids) are bids below four of the trump suit after partner makes a slam try. They are not legitimate cuebids, but merely say that you're interested (see page 216).

However, with something like:

♠ 10 8 4 2   ♡ K 7 5 3   ◇ 7 6   ♣ Q 7 3

partner signs off in 4♠ over your 4♣. The club queen is nice, but the poor trumps and wasted ♡K are slam-negative cards. In short, the first thing partner looks at is his trump holding.

Your hand again:

♠ K 6 5 3   ♡ —   ◇ A K Q 5 4 3   ♣ A K 4

On the second auction,

You	Partner
1◇	1♡
2♠	4♠

partner had:

♠ A Q 10 4   ♡ 10 7 5 3   ◇ 8 7 6   ♣ 7 3

After your jump shift, partner has nothing at all to tell you except that he has great trumps. Wow! In one bid your partner showed good trumps! You can bid the grand-slam force and play either six or seven with no risk.

Playing Fast Arrival, partner could have a huge variety of hands and you have to guess whether to go past game. Slow Arrival is the commonsense method, and you'll pick up lots of points when you manage to stop in game with poor trumps.

MINIMUM OR MAXIMUM?

Some 'minimums' are better than others:

Opener	Responder
♠ A J 6 5 3	♠ 8
♡ K 4 2	♡ A 8 6 5 3
◇ A 9	◇ K 5 2
♣ J 6 3	♣ A K Q 4
1♠	2♡
?	

Playing Fast Arrival, opener rebids 4♡ and responder is in the dark. Playing Slow Arrival, opener bids 3♡ and leaves room for partner to make a slam try with 4♣. Now opener can cooperate, because he has a nice hand within the context of his minimum! If we add the king of spades to opener's hand, he is good enough jump to 4♡, and responder would move toward slam.

Sometimes you bid slowly with a maximum because you want to set the trump suit in preparation for Keycard Blackwood, or a cuebid:

Opener	Responder
♠ A K 6 5 3	♠ 8
♡ K Q 4 2	♡ A J 6 5 3
◇ 7 3	◇ Q 5
♣ A 6	♣ K Q 7 5 4

1♠	2♡
3♡	4♡
5♣	5♡
pass	

Here both methods would probably create the same auction (though in Fast Arrival, responder might bid 4♣ over 3♡, since opener has shown extras).

TWO-OVER-ONE PLAYERS – THIS STUFF IS RIGHT UP YOUR ALLEY

Opener	Responder
1♠	2♡[1]
3♡	

1. Game-forcing.

Opener	Responder
1♠	2♡[1]
4♡	

1. Game-forcing.

If you play Fast Arrival, 3♡ shows extra values and 4♡ is weak. If you play Slow Arrival, 4♡ shows good trumps or good controls and 3♡ is weak or a hand that's heading past 4♡.

Notice that Slow Arrival caters to four types of hands (weak, good trumps, good controls, and super strong), while Fast Arrival only breaks down to weak or strong.

We began with this hand:

♠ 4 ♡ J 8 5 4 2 ◊ A K Q 6 3 ♣ A 4

Opener	Responder
1♠	2♡[1]
4♡	

1. Game-forcing.

Playing Fast Arrival, you have no idea what to do, but you'll probably pass 4♡, since partner showed a minimum. Playing Slow Arrival, you have an easy Blackwood or Keycard Blackwood continuation, because you know that partner has good trumps.

Here's another example. Opener holds:

♠ 5 ♡ A 8 4 3 ◊ A 6 5 4 3 ♣ A K 9

Opener	Responder
1◊	2♣[1]
2♡	?

1. Game forcing.

Let's look at how the auction might continue from here.

Opener	Responder #1
♠ 5	♠ A K
♡ A 8 4 3	♡ 7 6 5 2
◊ A 6 5 4 3	◊ K 8
♣ A K 9	♣ Q J 7 6 3

1◊	2♣[1]
2♡	3♡
4♣[2]	4♡[3]
pass	

1. Game-forcing.
2. Isn't it comforting to be able to make a slam try under game?
3. Must sign off because of the terrible trumps.

Opener	Responder #2
♠ 5	♠ A 6
♡ A 8 4 3	♡ K 6 5 2
◊ A 6 5 4 3	◊ K 8
♣ A K 9	♣ Q J 6 3 2

Opener	Responder #2
1♢	2♣[1]
2♡	3♡
4♣	4♢
4NT	5♢[2]
6♡	

1. Game forcing.
2. One ace.

Opener	Responder #3
♠ 5	♠ A 6
♡ A 8 4 3	♡ K Q 5 2
♢ A 6 5 4 3	♢ J 8
♣ A K 9	♣ Q J 6 3 2

1♢	2♣[1]
2♡	4♡
4NT	5♢[2]
5NT	6♢[3]
6♡	

1. Game-forcing.
2. One ace.
3. One King.

Finally, another great thing about Slow Arrival is that it allows you to find an alternative contract:

You	Partner
♠ A K 6 5 2	♠ —
♡ 9 3 2	♡ A K 6 5 4
♢ 2	♢ A K 7
♣ K Q 10 6	♣ A J 7 5 4

1♠	2♡[1]
3♡	4♣[2]
6♣	7♣
pass	

1. Game-forcing.
2. Natural.

The hearts are 3-2 and the clubs 3-1. In short, the breaks are normal enough, so the 6♡ bidders scored up their small slams, while you scored up your grand. On another day, you might score your 7♣ contract when the clubs are 2-2 and hearts 4-1, while the 6♡ contract goes down. Can the Fast Arrivalists reach 7♣, too? Perhaps, but it's much more difficult after

You	Partner
1♠	2♡
4♡	

Sounds like you're playing in hearts, right? Suppose the auction continues:

You	Partner
1♠	2♡
4♡	5♣
6♣	?

Partner doesn't have the same information about the clubs. When you jumped to 6♣ in the Slow Arrival auction, you showed great clubs. When you merely raise to 6♣, you can be weaker in clubs and partner might be tempted to play in his AKxxx suit rather than his AJxxx. In any event, why play a method where you are constantly guessing?

Here is a similar situation — this time Fast Arrival takes you right past your best contract:

Opener	Responder
♠ A K J 6 4	♠ Q 7
♡ 5 4 3	♡ Q 8 7 6 2
◇ J 5 2	◇ K Q 7
♣ A 6	♣ K J 4

1♠	2♡ [1]
4♡	

1. Game-forcing.

This is the popular 2/1 Fast Arrival auction. Opener goes fast to 4♡, usually down one or down two.

Using Slow Arrival, the auction goes:

Opener	Responder
1♠	2♡ [1]
3♡	3NT
pass	

1. Game-forcing.

Responder has the chance to suggest a different contract and opener is charmed to accept with his strong spades and weak heart holding.

Bread and Butter Conventions and Treatments

WHAT DO YOU LOSE BY PLAYING SLOW ARRIVAL?

Nothing, except that it's more advanced than Fast Arrival, and requires more thinking.

BEWARE: If you haven't discussed these auctions with your partner, he's probably playing Fast Arrival, the better-known method.

Bridge Conventions in Depth

Smolen

After partner has opened 1NT, it is difficult using Standard methods to bid hands that are 5-4 or 6-4 in the majors. Usually, whether you choose to use Stayman or Transfers, one of the suits is going to get lost or misdescribed. One solution is the **Smolen** convention.

Smolen is Stayman followed by a bid of three-of-a-major, after either a 1NT or 2NT opening bid. It shows four cards in the suit bid and five or six cards in the other major. When you use the Smolen Convention, you are going to game or slam. Here are the basic Smolen auctions:

Opener	Responder
1NT	2♣
2♢	3♡[1]

1. 5+ spades, 4 hearts.

Opener	Responder
1NT	2♣
2♢	3♠[1]

1. 5+ hearts, 4 spades.

Opener	Responder
2NT	3♣
3♢	3♡[1]

1. 5+ spades, 4 hearts.

Opener	Responder
2NT	3♣
3◇	3♠ [1]

1. 5+ hearts, 4 spades.

As well as being highly descriptive of hands that are hard to handle without this gadget, Smolen has the advantage of allowing opener, the stronger hand, to declare. For example, you, the responder, hold:

♠ A K 7 6 3   ♡ Q J 6 5   ◇ 3 2   ♣ 3 2

Partner	You
1NT	2♣
2◇ ?	

You have no tenace to protect, so there's no reason for you to declare. You know partner doesn't hold four of either major, but he might hold three-card spade support. You bid 3♡, your four-card major, in the hope that with three spades partner can bid them. If partner bids 3♠, you can bid 3NT, because you have a flat hand. Partner already knows you have five-four in the majors, and now he can decide where to play the hand.

Smolen also works after a 2♣ opening bid and a 2NT rebid. Again, it is important to have the strong hand declare the 5-3 fit. Amazingly, most duplicate players aren't aware that Smolen is operative in this situation (or even over a 2NT opening)!

ALERT!

Smolen is never used at the two-level:

Partner	You
1NT	2♣
2◇	2♡ or 2♠

Partner	You
1NT	2♣
2♡	2♠

Partner	You
1NT	2◇ [1]
2♡	2♠

1. Transfer

Almost everyone plays 'non-forcing' Stayman, which means that responder's new suit at the two-level is not forcing. In the first example, you probably have 5-4 shape in the majors and a weak hand. Once partner denies a four-card major, you bid your five-card major, to play, and partner will bid again only with an extraordinary hand (maximum and three-card support).

The second example can be used to show a specific hand: you have a five-card spade suit with 7-8 points. You don't have quite enough to transfer to 2♠ and then bid again. This treatment allows you to stay at the two-level when partner has a minimum. Obviously, you can't use this treatment for hearts because partner may respond 2♠ to your Stayman bid.

In the third example, you showed a five-card heart suit with your transfer to 2♡. Now 2♠ can become a relay to show a number of different hand types. For now, the 2♠ bid should be natural, showing 5-5 in the majors and not forcing. If you have a more intricate method, by all means use it, but make sure you and partner are on the same wavelength.

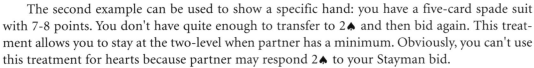

IN REAL LIFE

Here's an OKbridge example of why Smolen is so important:

East-West vul.

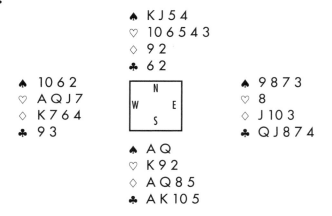

```
              ♠ K J 5 4
              ♡ 10 6 5 4 3
              ◇ 9 2
              ♣ 6 2
♠ 10 6 2                    ♠ 9 8 7 3
♡ A Q J 7      N            ♡ 8
◇ K 7 6 4    W   E          ◇ J 10 3
♣ 9 3          S            ♣ Q J 8 7 4
              ♠ A Q
              ♡ K 9 2
              ◇ A Q 8 5
              ♣ A K 10 5
```

West	North	East	South
			2NT
pass	3♣	dbl	redbl
pass	?		

At the table, North bid 3♡, natural, and played in 4♡ doubled, down one after the jack of diamonds opening lead.

Notice that if North-South play Smolen, North bids three spades instead, showing four spades and five hearts, and South declares four hearts doubled. From the South side, four hearts is cold.

Suppose West leads a club. Declarer wins and plays a heart. West wins and is helpless. If he plays ace and another heart, declarer wins, cashes his spades, plays a high club and ruffs a club, cashes dummy's spades, and eventually throws West in with his high heart. West must lead away from his king of diamonds. If West wins the first round of hearts and plays a spade, declarer wins and plays another heart. Declarer will eventually be able to pull trumps and take a club finesse (West will have to give dummy an entry in hearts or spades).

If West leads a spade, declarer must play a little differently. He wins, cashes the second spade, and plays a heart. If West wins and plays ace and another heart, declarer strips and end-plays him as before. If West wins and plays a third spade, declarer wins and plays a club, sticking in the ten if East plays low. Declarer then plays another heart and West must either clear hearts, providing declarer an entry for a second club play, or West has to play a minor suit, giving declarer a tenth trick.

Retransfers

One of the main reasons for using transfers over notrump openings is to ensure that the strong hand becomes declarer. Its strength will be concealed during the play, and the opening lead will come up to it, not through it. However, it is also useful to play, as many partnerships do, some form of pre-accept bid by opener to show a good fit and possible slam interest. What you now need, whether or not you are interested in slam exploration, is a way that you can still make the notrump bidder declarer eventually.

THE SOLUTION

There is a way. After you make a transfer bid, if partner does not accept the transfer, you can retransfer by bidding the suit below your suit (i.e., the same transfer-suit you bid the first time) at the next level.

The main reason for the retransfer is to ensure that the strong hand becomes declarer.

Opener	Responder
1NT	2◇
3♣	?

Here 2◇ was a transfer, while 3♣ was a pre-accept with a great hand for hearts and a doubleton club.

Responder can now retransfer with 3◇, then pass or continue bidding, depending on his hand. Either way, the strong hand is declarer.

Sometimes your transfer bid is doubled, which gives you some extra options:

Partner	Oppt	You	Oppt
1NT	pass	2♢	dbl
?			

Many play that passing the double shows a doubleton heart, while a bid of 2♡ shows a tripleton, allowing responder to compete more easily at the three-level if the next hand bids.

What if opener passes the double? For example, suppose you hold:

♠ 5 2   ♡ J 8 7 6 3 2   ♢ 9 6   ♣ 5 4 2

Partner	Oppt	You	Oppt
1NT	pass	2♢	dbl
pass	pass	?	

You can retransfer by redoubling. This does not mean you want to play 2♢ doubled and redoubled (if opener had redoubled it would have meant that). It means, 'Partner, please play this hand in 2♡.'

Finally, what does it mean if you don't retransfer, but instead bid your suit?

Opener	Responder
1NT	2♡[1]
2NT[2]	3♠

1. Transfer.
2. Pre-accept for spades.

Responder did not bid 3♡, the retransfer. One idea is to play that this bid means, 'Please cuebid — opposite your preaccept I think we have a slam!'

Opener	Oppt	Responder	Oppt
1NT	pass	2♡	dbl
pass	pass	3♠	

This time, responder wants to be declarer. Likely, he has a heart honor (perhaps the king) to protect. Of course, 3♠ is forcing — opener must raise or bid 3NT (taking into account the lead-directing double).

Sometimes, using a retransfer might help you reach a slam! Here's a real-life example:

Both vul.

                              ♠ K J 8 7 6 5 3
                              ♡ A
                              ◇ K Q 10
                              ♣ 8 2

    ♠ 9 4   N   ♠ 10 2
    ♡ 7 5 4   W   E   ♡ K J 10 9 6
    ◇ 8 4   S   ◇ 9 7 3 2
    ♣ A Q J 9 7 6   ♣ 5 3

                              ♠ A Q
                              ♡ Q 8 3 2
                              ◇ A J 6 5
                              ♣ K 10 4

West	North	East	South
			1NT
pass	2♡	dbl	pass
3♣	3♡[1]	pass	3♠
pass	4♡[2]	pass	6♠[3]
all pass			

1. Retransfer.
2. Cuebid/slam try.
3. A great spot – from the South hand.

Puppet Stayman

Suppose you pick up:

♠ J 6 4   ♡ 5 4   ◇ A J 10 2   ♣ 7 6 5 3

Partner opens 2NT. What is your response?

THE SOLUTION

The first convention we all probably learned was Stayman, so we all know how to locate 4-4 major fits after partner opens 1NT. But it's very common to open 2NT (and even 1NT these days) with a five-card major, and it's therefore important to have some method for pinpointing a 5-3 fit, especially if you have a ruffing value in the short hand.

The solution is **Puppet Stayman**. In this method, after a 2NT opening, 3♣ asks for a 5-card major. Puppet Stayman can also be played after a 1NT opening, but most players use it only after 2NT (or 2♣-2◇; 2NT).

There are a few different sets of responses for this convention, but one of the most popular is the following:

Opener	Responder
2NT	3♣
?	

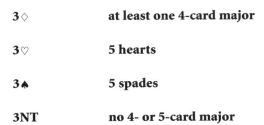

3◇	**at least one 4-card major**
3♡	**5 hearts**
3♠	**5 spades**
3NT	**no 4- or 5-card major**

Over a 3◇ bid, responder can:

1. Sign off in 3NT if he was looking only for a 5-card major.

2. Bid the major he does not hold with one 4-card major (allowing the strong hand to become declarer if there is a 4-4 major-suit fit).

3. Bid 4♣ with both majors.

4. Bid 4◇ with both majors and a slam try.

EXAMPLE #1

Opener	**Responder**
♠ K Q 7 6 2	♠ J 5 3
♡ K Q 8	♡ 7 4
◇ K Q 3	◇ A J 10 5
♣ A J	♣ 7 6 5 4
2NT	3♣
3♠	4♠

EXAMPLE #2

Opener	**Responder**
♠ A K 4	♠ Q 6 2
♡ K Q 6 5	♡ J 8 7 3
◇ K Q 2	◇ A 9 7 4
♣ A 7 6	♣ 3 2

Opener	Responder
2NT	3♣
3♢[1]	3♠[2]
4♡	pass

1. At least one four-card major.
2. Four hearts.

Alternative Auction:

Opener	Responder
♠ A K 4	♠ Q 6 2
♡ K Q 6 5	♡ J 8 7 3
♢ K Q 2	♢ A 9 7 4
♣ A 7 6	♣ 3 2

Opener	Responder
2NT	3♣
3♢[1]	3♠[2]
4♣[3]	4♢[4]
4♡	pass

1. At least one four-card major.
2. Four hearts.
3. Slam try in hearts.
4. Transfer back to hearts.

In the alternative second auction, opener, with a great hand and controls, decides to make a slam try over 3♠. He can do this by bidding 4♣, which is artificial and says, 'I have a maximum hand and a fit in hearts with you. If you have interest in slam, please go beyond 4♡.'

At this point, responder should bid 4♢, to transfer back to hearts, so that opener is the declarer. In our example, responder passed 4♡, because he did not have extra values for slam. But if he held the king of clubs in addition to his other high cards, he would press forward over 4♡ with a cuebid. This brings us to an important rule:

RETRANSFERS

Whenever the 4-4 trump fit is discovered and the suit has not yet been bid, responder should be careful not to bid the trump suit, but instead transfer to it. This ensures that the opener, with the strong hand, will become declarer.

Opener	Responder
♠ A 5 4	♠ J 8 7 3 2
♡ K 6	♡ A Q 5 4
◇ A K 6 3	◇ 8
♣ A Q 7 2	♣ 6 4 3
2NT	3♣
3NT	pass

When responder holds 5-4 in the majors, he may lose the 5-3 fit. (This is why many pairs use Smolen instead of Puppet Stayman.) One solution is to switch the 3♡ and 3NT responses to 3♣: play 3♡ as showing no major and 3NT as showing five hearts. Now the responses to 3♣ are as follows:

Opener	Responder
2NT	3♣
?	

3◇	**at least one 4-card major**
3♡	**no major**
3♠	**5 spades**
3NT	**5 hearts**

Over a 3NT rebid, responder should use 4◇ as a transfer to hearts. Over 3♡, responder can bid 3♠ with five spades and four hearts, so the partnership doesn't miss the 5-3 spade fit.

Opener	Responder
♠ K J 5	♠ A Q 7 2
♡ A K 6 5 3	♡ 9 4 2
◇ A Q 7	◇ 8 5 4 3
♣ A 2	♣ 6 5
2NT	3♣
3NT	4◇
4♡	pass

Here opener shows five hearts and responder signs off in game via a transfer bid.

The price for a comprehensive structure over partner's notrump opening, however, is that the more bids you make the more information you allow the opponents to exchange.

For example, look at this layout:

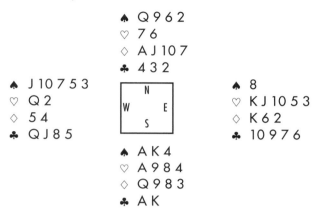

```
                    ♠ Q 9 6 2
                    ♡ 7 6
                    ◊ A J 10 7
                    ♣ 4 3 2
   ♠ J 10 7 5 3          N          ♠ 8
   ♡ Q 2          W          E      ♡ K J 10 5 3
   ◊ 5 4               S           ◊ K 6 2
   ♣ Q J 8 5                       ♣ 10 9 7 6
                    ♠ A K 4
                    ♡ A 9 8 4
                    ◊ Q 9 8 3
                    ♣ A K
```

With normal 2NT bidding, the auction goes:

West	North	East	South
			2NT
pass	3♣	pass	3♡
pass	3NT	all pass	

Club lead, diamond finesse loses, nine tricks. Or spade opening lead, and ten tricks.

Using Puppet Stayman, things are different:

West	North	East	South
			2NT
pass	3♣	pass	3◊ [1]
pass	3♡ [2]	dbl	3NT
all pass			

1. At least one 4-card major.
2. Four spades.

Heart lead, diamond finesse loses, down one.

Bridge Conventions in Depth

Moxe Slam Bidding After Stayman

Back on page 4, we described a useful method of making slam tries after a Stayman enquiry. After partner answers Stayman with a major-suit response, responder bids the other major at the three-level to show support of opener's major and a slam try. For example,

Partner	You
1NT	2♣
2♠	3♡[1]
?	

1. Slam try in spades.

Here are partner's rebids.

3♠	minimum
4♣, 4♢, 4♡	cuebid, interest in slam
4♠	minimum, but with great trumps (There is no other way to show this type of hand; a direct jump to 4♠ showing all minimums is not as informative. Therefore, we use 3♠ for most minimums, and 4♠ for the minimum with strong trumps.)
4NT	Blackwood (keycard for spades, if you play it

Partner	You
♠ K Q 7 5	♠ A 8 4 2
♡ A Q 2	♡ 6 5
◇ 10 6 4	◇ A J 5 2
♣ A J 2	♣ K Q 4 2
1NT	2♣
2♠	3♡[1]
4♣[2]	4◇[2]
4♡[2]	4♠
pass	

1. Slam try in spades.
2. Cuebid.

Partner obviously has a nice hand, but not quite enough to force to slam. Even if partner's queen of hearts were the queen of diamonds, you would need both the diamond finesse and a 3-2 spade break. To make a slam, you need a lot of luck, or the perfect hand from partner, for example:

♠ K Q 7 5   ♡ Q 3 2   ◇ K Q 4   ♣ A J 2

or

♠ K 8 7 3   ♡ A 3 2   ◇ K Q 6   ♣ A J 2

Another time when this gadget is useful is when you have enough to drive to slam yourself, but wish first to set up Keycard Blackwood (KCB). The first two rounds of bidding establish the trump suit:

You
♠ Q 4
♡ A 6 3 2
◇ A K Q 7
♣ Q 9 2

Partner	You
1NT	2♣
2♡	3♠[1]
4♡	4NT[2]

1. Slam try in hearts.
2. Keycard Blackwood for hearts.

We once had a similar hand and auction, and were the only pair to stay out of slam. Our entire auction went like this:

Matthew	Pamela
♠ A K 9	♠ Q 4
♡ J 8 5 4	♡ A 6 3 2
◊ J 10 3	◊ A K Q 7
♣ A K 3	♣ Q 9 2

1NT	2♣
2♡	3♠[1]
4♡	4NT[2]
5♡	pass[3]

1. Slam try in hearts.
2. Keycard Blackwood for hearts.
3. But not happy.

Matthew's 5♡ showed two key cards (out of five) without the queen of trumps. Pamela could see that we were off a keycard (an ace or the king of hearts) and the queen of hearts, making slam a poor bet.

OTHER SLAM TRIES AFTER STAYMAN

There are some additional ways to try for slam after the first Stayman response.

Opener	Responder
1NT	2♣
2♡	4♣ / 4◊
1NT	2♣
2♠	4♣ / 4◊

These jumps are traditionally played as a splinter bid, showing major-suit support, a singleton in the suit bid, and a slam try. Partner can bid 4NT, Blackwood (or Keycard Blackwood), or he can sign off in game, or, if possible, he can bid 'the suit in between':

Opener	Responder
1NT	2♣
2♡	4♣[1]
4◊	

1. Splinter.

Opener	Responder
1NT	2♣
2♠	4◊[1]
4♡	

1. Splinter.

You can use this bid as a cuebid, but we prefer to use the suit in between as a 'squeeze bid'. This means, 'If you have a maximum, I'm interested in slam, but I don't have quite enough to go past game by myself.' This bid is available for every sequence except:

Opener	Responder
1NT	2♣
2♡	4◇

This bid is also known as a 'Last Train Cuebid', named after the song *Last Train to Clarkesville*. (For more on this, see page 216.) Generally, you know whether or not you have a good hand without making the squeeze bid, but sometimes, despite holding a minimum, you have great trumps and you hate to sign off in game. After all, since you hold the great trumps, you know partner doesn't, and he'll be nervous about continuing past game with poor trumps.

By the way, Last Train only applies when there is only one cuebid available below the trump suit. (See the next sequence as an example with two cuebids available.)

Suppose you hold:

♠ K Q J 5   ♡ A 7   ◇ A 5 4 2   ♣ Q 6 3

You	Partner
1NT	2♣
2♠	4♣ [1]
?	

1. Splinter.

Here you can go ahead and bid a slam yourself. You have both red suits controlled, you have a ruffing value in your hand, and you have great trumps. What more can partner want?

On the other hand, suppose you hold:

♠ A K Q 3   ♡ J 5 2   ◇ K 4 3   ♣ K 3 2

This time you have the worst possible distribution and the wasted king of clubs. However, you might feel guilty about signing off with such great trumps after partner shows a singleton and makes a slam try. So over 4♣, you bid 4◇, a cuebid. If partner had splintered to 4◇, you would have made a 'squeeze bid' of 4♡.

As it turns out, partner has one of these two hands:

a)   ♠ 10 7 4 2   ♡ A K 6   ◇ A Q J 7 2   ♣ 5

b)   ♠ J 8 7 4   ♡ A Q 10 6   ◇ A Q 9 7 2   ♣ —

Both of these hands are lovely after finding the spade fit, but because of the poor trumps, it's not safe to go past the game level. After any squeak by the opener, however, it's only a question of good trumps for slam, and opener probably has them.

This brings us to the five-level. For this high-wire act, let's go to our bidding lab. . . .

Suppose you are bidding after Stayman or Jacoby Transfers, and suddenly one player bids the trump suit at the five-level. What in the world is that?

Example #1

Opener	Responder
1NT	2♡[1]
2♠	4♣[2]
4♠	5♠

1. Transfer.
2. Splinter.

Example #2

Opener	Responder
1NT	2♣
2♠	4♢[1]
4♠	5♠

1. Splinter.

Example #3

Opener	Responder
1NT	2♣
2♠	3♡[1]
4♠	5♠

1. Slam try for spades.

This isn't very scientific, but we like to play that the 5♠ bid means, 'Partner, please bid slam with any excuse.' (This principle can be used for many other bidding situations, which is why we like to use it here, keeping the bidding consistent.) The opener, having denied slam interest, can look again at his cards and bid slam with:

a) **trump honor(s)**

b) **ruffing value(s)**

c) **controls**

Let's look at some practical examples.
In Example #1, opener held:

♠ Q 6   ♡ A 5 2   ♢ Q 7 6 3   ♣ A K 5 4

The three quick tricks are nice, and the queen of spades is a good card, so having denied slam interest, you can go ahead and bid six. Partner held:

♠ K J 9 8 5 4 2   ♡ 7 4   ◇ A K 2   ♣ 3

In Example #2, opener held:

♠ J 6 5 4   ♡ K 8 2   ◇ A 5   ♣ A Q J 4

Opener passed the five-spade bid. If responder has a slam opposite this hand, with its poor trumps and massive club wastage, responder must bid it himself. Responder held:

♠ Q 1 0 7 3   ♡ A Q J 5 4   ◇ K 8 7 3   ♣ —

Responder couldn't bring himself to give up on slam after only one try, and who can blame him?

In Example #3, responder has all the room in the world to make slam tries, so what is he doing with the raise to 5♠? Well, we can deduce that he doesn't have shortness anywhere, or else he would have made a splinter bid, and he's not off too many aces or he would have bid Blackwood. So why is he torturing us? If we don't try to figure out every esoteric bid of partner's, and we instead stick to our rule of looking at our cards, we might say, well, whatever he wants 'I've got it' (or 'I don't have it'). Suppose opener has:

♠ Q 1 0 9 5   ♡ A 3   ◇ Q J 6 2   ♣ K Q J 5

Well, the first time around we showed our minimum values, but now, if partner is pushing, are we ashamed of our hand? On the one hand, we've got good trump spots and our honors are touching. On the other hand, we did open one notrump with a minimum point count and only two quick tricks. Let's be disciplined and pass. In fact, partner has:

♠ A J 6 3   ♡ K Q J 7 5   ◇ A 4   ♣ 6 2

Not a very good slam — good thing we passed (it would be a better contract if played from partner's side, avoiding the diamond lead through the ace). If our diamonds had been K-x-x-x instead of Q-J-x-x, we might have bid the slam, which would in fact then be on a spade finesse. With the hand we had, even five spades might go down.

Simple Keycard Blackwood Agreements

PREVIEW

Here's a fairly common situation where many partnerships go astray. You hold

♠ K Q J 10 5 3 2   ♡ 4   ◇ A 6 2   ♣ K 5

The auction goes:

Partner	You
1♡	1♠
4♡	?

If you bid 4NT here, and you are playing Keycard Blackwood, is this a Keycard situation, and if so, which is the 'key' suit?

THE SOLUTION

In regular Blackwood, there are four aces in the deck, and a player can ask how many of these four aces his partner has with a bid of Four Notrump. In Keycard Blackwood, there are five 'aces' — the four regular aces plus the king of trump. This is a very useful bid... as long as you know whether partner means the 4NT bid to be plain Blackwood or Keycard Blackwood, and as long as you know what the trump suit is! The late Victor Mitchell, considered by some to be the greatest bridge player of all time, refused to play Keycard Blackwood. He said that far more points are lost through keycard mix-ups than are gained by this convention. While this might not be true for the more sophisticated partnerships, it is certainly true for new partnerships and casual partnerships. Here is a simple statement of Keycard Blackwood agreements that is confusion-proof:

Blackwood is only Keycard Blackwood if a suit has been bid and raised. Not bid and 'implied', but bid and raised. So:

The raise can be in the form of an artificial bid (e.g., Jacoby 2NT, splinter bid, jump-shift-by-passed-hand-showing-a-fit, etc.). But it must clearly be a raise. So:

Partner	You
4♡	4NT[1]

1. Not Keycard.

Partner	You
1♡	1♠
3♡	4NT[1]

1. Not Keycard.

Partner	You
1♡	4♣
4♡	4NT[1]

1. This time it's Keycard because the splinter bid promises hearts.

Oppt	Partner	Oppt	You
3♠	4♡	pass	4NT[1]

1. Not Keycard.

While it's true that you may want 4NT to be Keycard in some of these situations, better safe than sorry (i.e,. no misunderstandings). In addition, suppose in the last example you held:

♠ 3   ♡ 9   ◇ A K Q J 10 9 8 3 2   ♣ K Q

What a sad story this might be if you weren't able simply to ask for aces! Nevertheless, this hand is rare, and some partnerships use a different rule:

If a suit has not been bid and raised, 4NT is Keycard Blackwood for the last bid suit.

If you choose to play this rule, rather than the simpler one, you may want to make the following exception: a jump to 4NT over partner's one-level opening bid is plain Blackwood. (After a one-level opening, you can usually make a forcing raise before using Keycard Blackwood.)

In addition to the above example, there is another reason why the 4NT bid over a one-level opening should not be Keycard Blackwood: because of the 'state of the match', or because you think you need a top on the last board to win a matchpoint event, you may wish to bid slam that is at best on a finesse. Suppose you hold:

♠ Q J 10 4   ♡ K Q 4   ◇ K 7   ♣ A Q 8 4

Your partner opens the bidding one spade. If you need a swing or are looking for a top score — you're happy to play in slam opposite any of these hands:

♠ A 9 8 3 2   ♡ A 8 3   ◇ Q J 10 2   ♣ 9

♠ A 9 8 3 2   ♡ 10 3   ◇ A Q 4   ♣ K 7 2

♠ A 9 8 3 2   ♡ 7 3 2   ◇ A J 4   ♣ K 7

In other words, you want to bid slam as long as they can't cash two aces. So you bid 4NT, plain Blackwood. (When you want to ask for Keycards, you begin with a forcing spade raise, and then bid Blackwood.)

Here's one that illustrates the 'last suit bid' rule:

Partner	You
1♡	1♠
4♡	4NT

Using 'last suit bid', 4NT is Keycard Blackwood for hearts, which is probably what responder wants it to be (unless he holds

♠ K Q J 10 5 3 2   ♡ 4   ◇ A 6 2   ♣ K 5

which is the hand we started off by showing you). Using the simpler rule (where you must raise first to make a Keycard Blackwood bid), this 4NT is plain Blackwood. It's true that you are probably going to play in hearts, but in order to keep the rules easy to remember and consistent, this is plain Blackwood. Can you miss anything? Not really. Suppose you have:

♠ A 9 8 3 2   ♡ Q 8   ◇ A K Q 3 2   ♣ 5

Again, the bidding goes

Partner	You
1♡	1♠
4♡	

You bid 4NT and partner shows two aces. Are you doomed because you don't know about the king of hearts (for a certainty)? No! There's an arcane bid that no one uses any more because Keycard Blackwood made it obsolete, and that bid is 6♣, Grand Slam Force in this situation. With two of the top three heart honors, partner bids seven. His hand was:

♠ 4   ♡ A K J 10 9 6 5 2   ◇ 5   ♣ A 5 2

Baby Blackwood

You pick up

♠ 5 ♡ K Q J 8 6 5 3 2 ◇ 3 ♣ A K J

Partner opens 1♠, next hand passes. What is your call? If you bid Blackwood, you are committing to the five-level opposite a partner who doesn't actually have to have any aces.

THE SOLUTION

Baby Blackwood is a neglected convention that is a great tool for checking for aces at a safe level. The double-jump response of 3NT is Blackwood. There's nothing else to it.

Opener	Responder
♠ K Q J 6 3 2	♠ 5
♡ 7	♡ K Q J 8 6 5 3 2
◇ K Q 10 7	◇ 3
♣ Q 6	♣ A K J

Opener	Responder
1♠	3NT
4♣[1]	4♡
pass	

1. 0 or 4 aces.

Even 4♡ is not iron-clad! Isn't it nice to know how many aces partner has below the five level?

Here's another example:

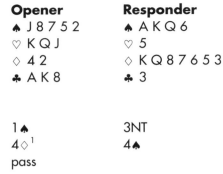

Opener	Responder
♠ J 8 7 5 2	♠ A K Q 6
♡ K Q J	♡ 5
◊ 4 2	◊ K Q 8 7 6 5 3
♣ A K 8	♣ 3

1♠	3NT
4◊¹	4♠
pass	

1. 1 ace.

This time you have a great fit with partner. As well, partner has an ace, but by stopping in 4♠ you might avoid a diamond ruff that defeats other pairs who reached 5♠.

Finally:

Opener	Responder
♠ 5	♠ A K Q J 8 6 3
♡ J 7 2	♡ K Q 5 4
◊ K Q J 6 3	◊ 5
♣ K Q 8 4	♣ 2

1◊	3NT
4♣¹	4♠
pass	

1. No aces.

Over a 4♡ reply, you can risk the slam. But it was nice to be able to stop in 4♠, wasn't it?

WHAT DO YOU LOSE BY PLAYING THIS CONVENTION?

The rare jump to 3NT over a one-bid. Surely you can find another way to bid a hand that wants to reach 3NT?

ADDITIONAL APPLICATION

Remember: Baby Blackwood applies only after a one-of-a-suit opening and without interference. However, you may wish to add this 3NT Baby to your repertoire:

Opener	Responder
1♠	3♠
3NT	

After a nine-card fit is established, the bid of 3NT is Baby Blackwood. Your hand for this might be something like:

♠ K Q J 6 5 2   ♡ 3   ♢ A K Q 5 4   ♣ 2

After opening 1♠ and hearing 3♠, why risk the five-level? Use Baby Blackwood instead.

DOPI and DEPO

PREVIEW

You pick up:

♠ 7 6   ♡ K J 7 5 4   ◇ A 6 2   ♣ K Q 3

You	Oppt	Partner	Oppt
1♡	3◇	4NT	5◇
?			

What is your call?

THE SOLUTION

It's not uncommon for opponents to bid in this kind of auction just to see whether you know what you're doing! The relevant agreements are called **DOPI** and **DEPO**. These two conventions are rare but when they come up they sure are important.

DOPI is played at the five-level after one partner bids Blackwood and the next opponent bids at the five-level.

DEPO is used when the opponent jumps to the six-level over 4NT.

These conventions apply even if you use Keycard Blackwood (where the trump king is counted as one of the aces).

DOPI

DOPI (Double 0 Pass 1) goes like this:

- **Double with 0 aces**
- **Pass with 1 ace**
- **Bid steps up the line with more**

In our example auction,

You	Oppt	Partner	Oppt
1♡	3◇	4NT	5◇
?			

Double	0 aces
Pass	1 ace
5♡	2 aces
5♠	3 aces

If you are playing Roman Keycard Blackwood, the replies would be:

Double	0 or 3 keycards
Pass	1 or 4 keycards
5♡	**2 keycards without the queen of trumps**
5♠	**2 keycards with the queen of trumps**

If you play 1430 responses (where 5♣ shows one or four and 5◇ shows zero or three), you should drop them after interference; otherwise you are playing PODI (or DIPO)!

Another point about Keycard Blackwood: you must first agree whether the jump to 4NT is Keycard Blackwood, since you haven't agreed on a trump suit yet (see page 106). We'll assume for now that 4NT in our example auction is Keycard Blackwood for hearts.

Let's go back to the preview:

♠ 7 6   ♡ K J 7 5 4   ◇ A 6 2   ♣ K Q 3

You	Oppt	Partner	Oppt
1♡	3◇	4NT	5◇
?			

If 4NT was simple Blackwood, you pass, showing one ace.
If 4NT was Keycard Blackwood, you bid 5♡, showing two keycards without the queen.

DEPO

DEPO (Double Even, Pass Odd) goes as follows:
- **Double with an even number of aces**
- **Pass with an odd number of aces**

You	Oppt	Partner	Oppt
1♠	3♣	4NT	6♣
?			

Double	**0, 2, or 4 aces**
Pass	**1 or 3 aces**

Using Keycard Blackwood, your possible bids would look like this:

Double	**0, 2, or 4 keycards**
Pass	**1 or 3 keycards**

This is an easy method, but has probably not been examined closely by partnerships. After all, with four aces (or four keycards) don't you want to be in slam if partner is asking for aces? In fact, with three aces you probably want to be in slam, so why make the opener guess? We suggest that if a small slam is still possible (this means that their bid is below your trump suit at the six-level), use DEPO with fewer than three aces, and make a 'step' bid with three or more.

You	Oppt	Partner	Oppt
1♠	3♣	4NT	6♣
?			

In this auction, then:

Double	**0 or 2**
Pass	**1**
6♦	**3**
6♥	**4**

Bread and Butter Conventions and Treatments

EXTRA

Use DOPI when the opponent bids over Gerber. In a world-class event a few years ago, it was reported that two world-renowned partnerships reached 7NT doubled on these cards:

	Opener	Responder
♠	K J 8 7	Q
♡	A Q 4	K J 6
◊	A 10 6	7
♣	Q 10 3	A K J 9 8 7 4 2

Opener	Oppt	Responder	Oppt
1NT	pass	4♣	4◊
?			

Fourth seat bid 4◊ over 4♣. Now there was confusion, as opener didn't know how to show two aces. The solution is easy. Play DOPI: opener bids 4♡ to show two aces.

ANOTHER IDEA

Add ROPI to your list of conventions for interference over Blackwood or Gerber.

You	Oppt	Partner	Oppt
1NT	pass	4♣	dbl
?			

When 4♣ has been doubled, redouble to show zero, pass to show one and bid up the line with two or more, just like with DOPI. It's the same method, except instead of doubling to show zero, you redouble to show zero.

WHAT DO YOU LOSE BY PLAYING THIS CONVENTION?

You can't double the opponents to show that you have a bad hand and simply want to stop partner from bidding. On the other hand, partner didn't ask you about your hand quality — partner asked for aces. Once he knows you have none, he can always pass your double for penalties if he wishes.

Italian Cuebids

PREVIEW

You pick up:

♠ J 10 6 3   ♡ A K Q 2   ◇ 5 4   ♣ J 10 6

Partner opens 1♠. You make a limit raise of 3♠. Partner bids 4◇ (cuebid). What is your call?

THE SOLUTION

It may seem obvious to cuebid 4♡, but as always, it depends on what the implications of partner's failure to cuebid clubs are.

The Italian systems of the 1950s and 1960s popularized a style of cuebidding where you cuebid first- or second-round controls (aces, kings, voids, singletons) indiscriminately. Combined with Blackwood or Keycard Blackwood, it makes an effective slam investigatory method.

One of the advantages of this method is that you can locate a suit where the partnership is off the first two tricks, and stop on a dime in game. For example:

Opener	Responder
♠ A Q 5 2	♠ K J 10 7 6 3
♡ J 6 5	♡ 10 9 4
◇ A K 4 3	◇ Q J
♣ Q 9	♣ A K

Opener	Responder
1NT	2♡[1]
3♠	4♣
4◇	4♠
pass	

1. Transfer.

Responder transfers to spades; opener shows four trumps. Responder cuebids 4♣; opener cuebids 4◇, and responder bids 4♠, denying either first- or second-round heart control. The partnership stops just in time.

Opener	Responder
♠ K Q 7 2	♠ A J 6 5 4
♡ K Q	♡ 8 6
◇ 5 3	◇ A 9 2
♣ A Q 6 5 2	♣ K J 7

Opener	Responder
1♣	1♠
3♠	4♣
4♡	4NT
5♠	6♠

Responder learns about the heart control at the four-level and can bid Keycard Blackwood, locating two keycards and the trump queen, just enough for slam.

One of the important points about Italian cuebids is that when partner skips a suit, denying a control in that suit, you must sign off immediately if you don't have a control either. Let's look at the opening preview hand.

♠ J 10 6 3   ♡ A K Q 2   ◇ 5 4   ♣ J 10 6

Partner opens 1♠. You make a limit raise of 3♠. Partner bids 4◇. What is your call?

Partner's 4◇ bid has denied a club control, so you must bid 4♠. A bid of 4♡ would promise that you held a club control, since you know partner doesn't.

Partner held:

♠ A K Q 7 5 2   ♡ 10   ◇ A K Q   ♣ 8 5 3

It would be great to be able to stop in 4♠, wouldn't it?

You lose the natural slam try in a new suit. For example, if you belong in slam in a different suit than your first agreed trump suit, you might not be able to find this fit:

Opener	Responder
♠ A K 7 6 4	♠ Q J 8 5
♡ A 8	♡ 4 3
◇ Q J 7 2	◇ A K 5 3
♣ A 7	♣ J 8 4

1♠	3♠
4◇	6◇
pass	

Simple, old-fashioned bidding reaches the best spot. Six spades is down one but six diamonds makes when diamonds are 3-2.

You also lose when you tell the opening leader what to lead or how to defend, because you gave away in the bidding where your weakness is. For example:

Opener	Responder
♠ A 7 6 4	♠ K 9 8 5 3
♡ 5	♡ A K 6 2
◇ Q 8 2	◇ 6 5 4
♣ A Q J 6 3	♣ K

1♣	1♠
3♠	4♣
4♡	4♠
pass	

Good stop, but the opening leader has the KJx of diamonds and the QJ10 of hearts and leads a diamond, knowing that's your weakness. Trumps are 3-1 so you go down one. Or trumps are 2-2, but after they cash three diamond tricks a fourth round of diamonds is led and ruffed by an opponent, promoting a trump trick for them.

Even if they take only three diamond tricks, you'd get a poor score at matchpoints. Meanwhile, the player who simply bids 6♠ over 3♠ without the cuebidding gets a heart lead and wraps up the slam. (Of course, even playing Italian Cuebids, you can choose not to go through the motions, and just shoot the slam.)

Bread and Butter Conventions and Treatments

The Forcing Pass

Forcing Passes usually occur when the partnership is in a game-forcing auction and the opponents sacrifice. The pass forces partner either to make another bid or double the opponents. **East-West vul.**

West	North	East	South
1♡	1♠	2♠	4♠
pass			

Because East cuebid 2♠, East-West must be going to game (assume that a jump to 3♡ would have been a limit raise, and the cuebid is a game force). Thus, after South sacrifices in four spades, West's pass is a Forcing Pass.

West does not want to double 4♠, perhaps because he has shortness there and extra distribution. For example:

♠ 5   ♡ K Q 7 5 2   ◇ A 6 3   ♣ K J 6 4

So far, most players will have a good understanding of the situation. But what happens next? What does it mean when you bid now as against when you pass (forcing) and then bid over partner's double? Here are the two cases:

Auction #1

West	North	East	South
1♡	2◇	3◇	5◇
5♡			

Auction #2

West	North	East	South
1♡	2◇	3◇	5◇
pass	pass	dbl	pass
5♡			

Some play that a direct 5♡ bid (Auction #1) is merely competitive, with extra distribution, while the 'slow' 5♡ bid (Auction #2) is stronger, inviting a slam. (Had East bid 5♡ instead of doubling, presumably West would have bid six.)

The reverse agreement — pass is always the weaker action — probably works better because if you play that 'pass and pull' shows a good hand, you can run into ethical problems if your partner doubles slowly. If you have a mild slam try, you bid directly and show 'extras'. For example, you, West, hold:

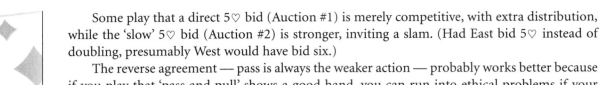

♠ A 5   ♡ A J 10 6 5 4   ◊ 7   ♣ A 8 3 2

West	North	East	South
1♡	2◊	3◊	5◊
5♡			

You don't need much from partner for a slam in hearts, and you save yourself from this unpleasant scenario:

West	North	East	South
1♡	2◊	3◊	5◊
pass[1]	pass	dbl[2]	pass
??[3]			

1. Planning to pull the double to show extras.
2. After a long hesitation.
3. Uh-oh; the opponents are already glaring at you. If this were a tournament, you'd be wondering if you can win your case at the committee, which will take place at 1:00 a.m., at which time you were hoping to be asleep.

However, if your agreement is that pass is always the weakest call, and you pull partner's double on the above auction, you'll have something like:

♠ Q 5 2   ♡ A K Q 6 5 4 3   ◊ —   ♣ Q 6 5

No one in his right mind would defend 5◊ with this hand, which might easily be a make (in fact, it might be a double game swing). No ethical problems; no committee. Even if partner takes an hour to double, you can pull with a clear conscience. This happened in real life, and the whole deal was:

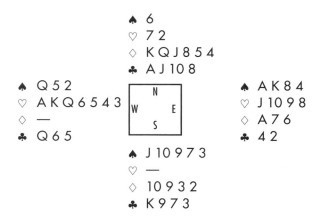

♠ 6
♡ 7 2
◇ K Q J 8 5 4
♣ A J 10 8

♠ Q 5 2
♡ A K Q 6 5 4 3
◇ —
♣ Q 6 5

♠ A K 8 4
♡ J 10 9 8
◇ A 7 6
♣ 4 2

♠ J 10 9 7 3
♡ —
◇ 10 9 3 2
♣ K 9 7 3

West	North	East	South
1♡	2◇	3◇	5◇
pass	pass	dbl	pass
5♡	pass		

They make 5◇ and you make 5♡. They have a one-down sacrifice in 6◇, but let them find it after they were doubled in 5◇!

FORCING PASSES AT LOW LEVELS

West	North	East	South
1♣	1♠	pass	2♣
dbl	?		

In this case, North-South are not going to play in a doubled cuebid, so this is a Forcing Pass situation.

North could pass or bid 2♠ directly over the double. Many play that the direct 2♠ bid is weaker than the pass, but again, pass as the weakest action works better. If you pass with a minimum, you save space. Your partner can now make a further descriptive game try with a bid of 2◇ or 2♡. If you bid 2♠, to show a weak hand, you've preempted your own auction!

Use the direct 2♠ bid here to show a six-card spade suit, and a non-minimum (but not enough to force to game, since 2♠ is not forcing). Partner can make a further game try at the three-level in safety.

West	East
♠ K 5 4	♠ A Q 10 7 2
♡ A Q 10 7 6	♡ K 5 2
◇ 4 2	◇ 8 7 5 3
♣ K 8 3	♣ 6

When pass is always the weakest call, the auction goes:

West	North	East	South
	1♣	1♠	pass
2♣	dbl	pass	pass
2♡	pass	3♡	pass
4♡	all pass		

West thinks he is protecting his ♣K, but ten tricks are always cold, assuming the majors break. Suppose 2♠ was the weakest call:

West	North	East	South
	1♣	1♠	pass
2♣	dbl	2♠	pass
?			

What should West do? Should he risk another bid? It looks like his ♣K is a wasted card (it is), so where is he going opposite a minimum?

In a higher-level auction, too, 'pass is the weakest call' is a space saver. Suppose your side is bidding spades and their side is bidding one of the minors; your Forcing Pass, showing the weak hand, gives partner another chance to make one last slam try, for example:

West	North	East	South
1♠	2◇	3◇	5◇
pass	pass	5♡	

West	North	East	South
1♠	2♣	3♣	5♣
pass	pass	5◇ or 5♡	

East might have a hand that makes slam opposite certain minimums.

TO SUM UP

1. A Forcing Pass applies at the four-level or higher when you or partner has bid or invited game and one of you has (a) cuebid, or (b) made a strong response, such as a 2-over-1 or a limit raise, or (c) has bid two suits.
2. Pass is the weakest call in any competitive auction.
3. The rules for the Forcing Pass also apply when the opponents double your cuebid at any level.

Pass in Competition = Weakest Action

If you've already read the previous section on the Forcing Pass, our recommendation that, in competition, 'pass' should always be the weakest action will not come as a shock. A free bid, when a pass is forcing, shows extra values:

West	North	East	South
1◇	dbl	pass	1♡
pass	2◇	dbl	?

Partner cuebid and East gave you extra bidding room by doubling. Thank him and make one of the following calls:

1) **Pass** is the weakest hand, or waiting (i.e., nothing to say at the moment)
2) **Redouble** shows a maximum for the previous bidding, but probably denies five hearts. You have something like:

    ♠ 5 2   ♡ A Q 6 3   ◇ J 7 6 2   ♣ J 10 7

3) **2♡** promises five hearts and a little extra:

    ♠ 5 2   ♡ A Q 7 6 3   ◇ 7 6 2   ♣ 7 6 5

Here's another example:

West	North	East	South
1♣	1♠	pass	2♠
pass	3♣	dbl	?

Again, the opponents have given you a free pass to show weakness:

1) **Pass** is the weakest hand
2) **Redouble** is a maximum for previous bidding
3) **3♠** is not the worst hand or you would have passed; probably something extra in trumps
4) **3◇ or 3♡** shows values here; not enough to bid game yourself, though:

♠ Q 5 3　♡ 6 5　◇ K Q J 7 4　♣ 8 3 2

or

♠ J 5 3　♡ A Q J 4　◇ 7 6 4　♣ 8 3 2

This also works at higher levels:

West	North	East	South
1♠	pass	4◇[1]	dbl
?			

1. Splinter.

When South doubles, West thanks him and passes to say he has no interest in slam. Responder now has extra room to make a further slam try (with a 4♡ bid) under the level of game. If, however, you play that 4♠ is the weakest rebid, East must go to the five-level to explore slam (he might have a slam try even opposite a minimum).

South	West	North	East
1♠	2♡	3♡[1]	4♡
pass			

1. Game force in spades.

South passes to say that he does not have anything to say. By using pass as the weakest action (instead of bidding 4♠), you allow your partner the luxury of doubling them! Look at this deal:

North-South vul.

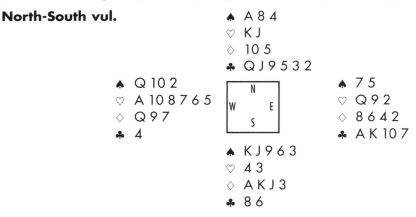

At most tables, the auction will go like this:

West	North	East	South
			1♠
2♡	3♡	4♡	4♠
all pass			

Result: down 1, for –100 North-South.

At your table, however, things will be different:

West	North	East	South
			1♠
2♡	3♡	4♡	pass
pass	dbl	all pass	

North leads the ace of spades and shifts to a diamond. South plays three rounds of diamonds. North ruffs the third diamond, plays a spade to South's king and now is able to score his king of hearts on the fourth round of diamonds! So the defense take six tricks for +500.

The corollary to these weak passes is that a free bid invites further bidding!

West	North	East	South
			1♠
2♡	3♡	4♡	4♠

This time South has:

♠ A K Q 7 6 2   ♡ 5   ◇ K 6 3   ♣ J 5 4

The four-spade bid shows something good in spades and is stronger than a pass. North's hand:

♠ 8 5 4 3   ♡ 6 2   ◇ A Q J 8 2   ♣ A 7

He can bid 5♠ over 4♠ to ask for a heart control for slam, and the laydown slam is reached.

This method also shows the value of playing the 3♡ cuebid by partner as a game force (rather than as game-invitational or better), and retaining 3♠ as the limit raise.

Bridge Conventions in Depth

Landy

There must be dozens of conventions designed to help you compete over an opponent's 1NT opening, but you'd be surprised how many experts play a simple old favorite: **Landy**. After an opponent opens 1NT, a 2♣ overcall is Landy, showing both majors (in direct or balancing seat).

Ideally you should have 5-5 in the majors and a good hand to bid Landy. However, you may wish to compete in the bidding with a weak hand and long majors, or a decent hand with 4-5 or 5-4 in the majors, especially at favorable vulnerability. Therefore, you need some 'machinery' so that you can land in the best fit, the 5-2 instead of the 4-2 major-suit fit, or even in a minor suit when appropriate. The full Landy treatment is:

Oppt	Partner	Oppt	You
1NT	2♣	pass	2♦

The 2♦ response to Landy shows equal length in the majors (2-2 or 3-3) and asks partner to choose his longer major.

WHEN THEY DOUBLE LANDY

Oppt	Partner	Oppt	You
1NT	2♣	dbl	?

pass	club length; let's play in two clubs, doubled
2♦	diamond length; let's play in two diamonds
2♡	2♠ to play
redbl	please bid your better major, partner; I have equal length in the majors
anything else	to play

Since no cuebid is available to suggest a game try, a jump in either major is a natural game try:

Oppt	Partner	Oppt	You
1NT	2♣	dbl	3♡/3♠[1]

1. These bids promise 4 trumps

Your game tries will depend on the vulnerability. For example:

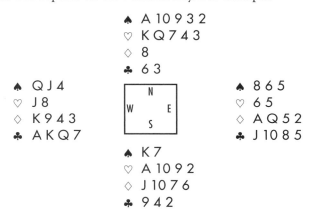

West	North	East	South
1NT	2♣	pass	?

If North-South are not vulnerable (especially not-vulnerable against vulnerable), South bids 3♡, a game try. North accepts because he is five-five, his honors are in his suits, and he has top honors rather than secondary honors. If, however, North-South are vulnerable (especially vulnerable against not-vulnerable), South bids 4♡. He is certain that his partner has a decent hand, he is happy to bid game because of his four-card heart suit and great spade holding. In the example hand, both spades and hearts break, but this game requires that only one of the major suits breaks evenly, and even if both break badly declarer has chances for ten tricks.

Sometimes you'll want to invite game with only three-card support:

♠ A 9 4   ♡ 2   ◇ A 9 8 4 2   ♣ A J 6 2

Oppt	Partner	Oppt	You
1NT	2♣	pass	?

You clearly want to be in game opposite anything other than a 'rag'. What to do? Bid 2NT, asking. You can agree on various responses with your favorite partner, but one set of step-responses is this:

Oppt	Partner	Oppt	You
1NT	2♣	pass	2NT
pass	?		

3♣	medium strength, 4-5 or 5-4
3♢	maximum strength, 4-5 or 5-4
3♡	5-5 'rag'
3♠	5-5 medium strength
3NT	5-5 maximum strength

Over 3♣, South bids 3♢ to ask for the five-card major, or he can bid three-of-a-major to invite.

Over 3♢, South bids his own 3-card major, game-forcing. North raises with 5-card support, or rebids 3NT. Notice that the Landy bidder has a 'rag' only when 5-5 – don't bid on poor hands with only 5-4 shape.

Here's a full deal example:

Both vul.

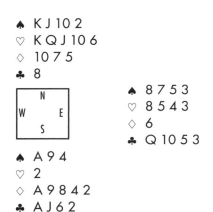

```
                        ♠ K J 10 2
                        ♡ K Q J 10 6
                        ◇ 10 7 5
                        ♣ 8
        ♠ Q 6                           ♠ 8 7 5 3
        ♡ A 9 7          N              ♡ 8 5 4 3
        ◇ K Q J 3    W       E          ◇ 6
        ♣ K 9 7 4        S              ♣ Q 10 5 3
                        ♠ A 9 4
                        ♡ 2
                        ◇ A 9 8 4 2
                        ♣ A J 6 2
```

On this deal, the auction goes:

West	North	East	South
1NT	2♣	pass	2NT
pass	3♣[1]	pass	3◇[2]
pass	3♡	pass	3NT[3]
all pass			

1. Medium strength, 4-5 or 5-4.
2. Which is your 5-card major?
3. OK, we'll play here, then.

Your definition of medium or maximum will depend on your agreement about the strength of the Landy overcall. We prefer overcalling with fairly strong hands when we are 5-4 or 4-5 (which is why North's hand bids 3♣ here, showing a medium hand). With 5-5 distribution and favorable vulnerability, we play the 'green-light' rule and anything goes. As long as partner is aware of what you're doing, he'll make his game tries accordingly. However, before you make a Landy bid, keep in mind that if you don't buy the hand, you have given the opponents a blueprint of the distribution when they play their contract. As our friend Victor Mitchell once said when asked which convention he preferred over 1NT, 'That depends. Who's got the rest of the deck, my partner or my LHO?'

Specific Suits Michaels

PREVIEW

You pick up

♠ 8 7 3 2   ♡ K 4   ◇ A J 5 3 2   ♣ 8 3

Your LHO opens 1♠. Partner bids 2♠, and RHO bids 4♠. What is your call?

What was 2♠? Let's assume it was the very popular Michaels convention, showing hearts and a minor.

This bidding problem shows a big flaw in the Michaels convention. Fourth seat must pass 4♠ or risk disaster at the five-level if partner has hearts and clubs. But what if partner has hearts and diamonds?

THE SOLUTION

It is much easier to play that the cuebid of a major-suit opening shows two specific suits. That way fourth seat knows how to handle the auction.

Some people use an 'Upper 2 Suits Cuebid', where the cuebid shows the top two unbid suits. In our example, the 2♠ cuebid would show hearts and diamonds. Another version is 'Color Cuebids':

Oppt	Partner	Oppt	You
		1♠	2♠

The red suits: hearts and diamonds.

Oppt	Partner	Oppt	You
		1♡	2♡

The black suits: spades and clubs.

In either case, you can play that it shows 5-5 shape, as in the regular Michaels convention, or you can use it to show 4-6 shape with a four-card major and six-card minor. Interestingly, it's safer to use the two-suited cuebid with 4-6, since you're more likely to have a safe harbor with a six-card suit.

HOW MANY POINTS DO YOU NEED FOR THIS BID?

Points, shmoints. If you have the suits, and you are watching the vulnerability, you can use your discretion.

In the Preview example, if your cuebid shows the red suits, fourth hand has an easy 5◊ bid. The full deal was:

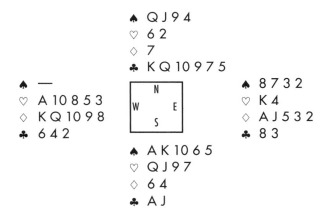

```
                    ♠ Q J 9 4
                    ♡ 6 2
                    ◇ 7
                    ♣ K Q 10 9 7 5
♠ —                                    ♠ 8 7 3 2
♡ A 10 8 5 3         N                 ♡ K 4
◇ K Q 10 9 8    W         E            ◇ A J 5 3 2
♣ 6 4 2              S                 ♣ 8 3
                    ♠ A K 10 6 5
                    ♡ Q J 9 7
                    ◇ 6 4
                    ♣ A J
```

West	North	East	South
			1♠
2♠	4♠	5◇	?

From this point on, East-West have a winning position, since they make 5◇ while North-South have only ten tricks in spades.

Another example:

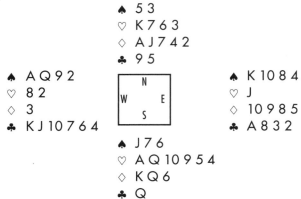

```
                        ♠ 5 3
                        ♡ K 7 6 3
                        ◇ A J 7 4 2
                        ♣ 9 5
   ♠ A Q 9 2                          ♠ K 10 8 4
   ♡ 8 2            N                 ♡ J
   ◇ 3        W           E           ◇ 10 9 8 5
   ♣ K J 10 7 6 4      S              ♣ A 8 3 2
                        ♠ J 7 6
                        ♡ A Q 10 9 5 4
                        ◇ K Q 6
                        ♣ Q
```

West	North	East	South
			1♡
2♡	3♡	4♠	?

In one bid, West tells East that his hand contains ten black cards, and East is in an excellent position to judge the auction.

RESPONDING TO SPECIFIC SUITS MICHAELS

All bids in our suits are natural and not forcing. A cuebid invites game and shows 3-card support for the major. After third hand raises opener's suit, double can be used to show the invitational hand with 3-card major-suit support.

Competitive Bidding after a Strong 2♣ Opening

PREVIEW

North-South vul.
You, South, hold:

♠ A K Q 9   ♡ A 8 6 3   ◇ K Q 3   ♣ A 5

West	North	East	South
			2♣
pass	2◇	3♡	?

Noting that double here is a penalty double, what would you do?

THE SOLUTION

You really have no alternative except to pass. It's true that you seem to have five tricks against 3♡, but your hand can easily be worth much more than +100. You don't have 'wastage' in hearts, so your hand is very good for offense. What should you do?

The answer is that you pass. This is a Forcing Pass: even with a terrible hand, responder must bid. A double by responder at his turn, by the way, is also a penalty double (although in this situation, since your pass is forcing, his double might be forced on a 4-3-3-3 yarborough —it doesn't show real values or hearts).

If you pass, the bidding continues:

West	North	East	South
			2♣
pass	2◇	3♡	pass
pass	4♡	pass	4♠
all pass			

Responder wasn't thrilled about cuebidding with a three-count, but he did have nice shape.

```
              ♠ 6 5 4 3
              ♡ —-
              ◇ 10 7 4 2
              ♣ K 10 8 7 4
              ┌─────────┐
              │    N    │
              │ W     E │
              │    S    │
              └─────────┘
              ♠ A K Q 9
              ♡ A 8 6 3
              ◇ K Q 3
              ♣ A 5
```

A Forcing Pass by the opening 2♣ bidder tends to show a 22-24 HCP notrump hand. Therefore, responder can make a penalty double with only three trumps:

North-South vul.

```
                        ♠ J 4 2
                        ♡ Q J 6
                        ◇ K 10 9 2
                        ♣ J 9 6
   ♠ Q 9 8 5      ┌─────────┐      ♠ 10 3
   ♡ 4            │    N    │      ♡ A K 9 8 5 2
   ◇ J 7 6 5 3    │ W     E │      ◇ 8 4
   ♣ 10 8 7       │    S    │      ♣ 5 3 2
                  └─────────┘
                        ♠ A K 7 6
                        ♡ 10 7 3
                        ◇ A Q
                        ♣ A K Q 4
```

West	North	East	South
			2♣
pass	2◇	2♡	pass
pass	dbl	all pass	

East slipped in a lead-directing 2♡ bid at favorable vulnerability, and lived to regret it. North-South can make at least ten tricks in notrump, but with good defense they can score +800 against two hearts doubled.

Competitive Bidding after a Strong 2♣ Opening

Defense to Bergen Raises

32

PREVIEW

Bergen Raises are specialized raises of opener's major-suit opening bid. After the opening bidder starts with one heart or one spade and the next hand passes, his partner bids:

Oppt	Partner	Oppt	You
1♠	pass	2♠	?

6-9 HCP with three-card support.

Oppt	Partner	Oppt	You
1♠	pass	3♣	?

6-9 with four-card support.

Oppt	Partner	Oppt	You
1♠	pass	3♦	?

10-11 with four-card support.

Oppt	Partner	Oppt	You
1♠	pass	3♠	?

Preemptive: 0-5 points with 4 trumps.

3♣ and 3♦, then, are totally artificial. Some partnerships invert the meanings of the 3♣ and 3♦ bids, making 3♣ the stronger one, but that doesn't affect our proposed defense in any way.

Bergen Raises allow the opening bidder's side to jack up the auction quickly to the three-level any time they have a 9-card fit!

Oppt	Partner	Oppt	You
1♠	pass	2♠	dbl

Oppt	Partner	Oppt	You
1♠	pass	3♠	dbl

Double of a raise is, as usual, takeout.

Oppt	Partner	Oppt	You
1♠	pass	3♣ / 3♦	pass
3♠	pass	pass	dbl

If responder bids three clubs or three diamonds and you (in fourth position) have a strong hand with shortness in the opener's major, you can pass, wait for the opponents to return to their major, and then double for takeout.

Oppt	Partner	Oppt	You
1♠	pass	3♦	3♠

A cuebid of the opener's major shows a strong 5-5 hand, five cards in the unbid major and five cards in a minor.

Oppt	Partner	Oppt	You
1♠	pass	3♣	dbl

Double of 3♣ shows five or more clubs, and four or more of the other major.

Oppt	Partner	Oppt	You
1♠	pass	3♦	dbl

Double of 3♦ shows five or more diamonds, and four or more of the other major.

Oppt	Partner	Oppt	You
1♠	pass	3♣	3♦

A 3♦ bid over their 3♣ bid shows five-plus diamonds and four or more of the other major. Examples:

♠ A 6 3 2   ♡ 8 4   ◇ 7 6   ♣ A K J 5 4

Oppt	Partner	Oppt	You
1♡	pass	3♣[1]	dbl[2]

1. Bergen Raise.
2. 5+ clubs and four of the other major (spades).

♠ A Q 7 6 2　♡ 8 4　◇ 6　♣ A K 7 3 2

Oppt	Partner	Oppt	You
1♡	pass	3♣[1]	3♡[2]

    1. Bergen Raise.
    2. Spades and a minor, 5/5.

♠ A Q 6 2　♡ 5　◇ K 6 4　♣ A K 7 3 2

Oppt	Partner	Oppt	You
1♡	pass	3♣[1]	pass
3♡	pass	pass	dbl[2]

    1. Bergen Raise.
    2. Takeout.

♠ A K 6 2　♡ 5 4　◇ A J 10 6 4 3　♣ 7

Oppt	Partner	Oppt	You
1♡	pass	3♣[1]	3◇[2]

    1. Bergen Raise.
    2. 5+ diamonds, four spades.

♠ A K 6 2　♡ 5 4　◇ A J 10 6 4 3　♣ 7

Oppt	Partner	Oppt	You
1♡	pass	3◇[1]	dbl[2]

    1. Bergen Raise.
    2. 5+ diamonds, four spades.

WHAT DO YOU GIVE UP?

You lose the ability to double their minor for a lead, or to bid 3◇ naturally over 3♣, but you can show four of the other major when you have it without much risk (i.e., if you hit partner with the wrong hand, the opponents aren't likely to be able to do much about it!).

The Best Defense to Multi

33

When they spring the dreaded Multi Two Diamonds upon you, are you ready to punish them for their ugly five-card suit weak two-bid, which is what they often have when using this convention?

Most defenses to Multi are attempts to get into the auction and survive. But Jeff Rubens, of *The Bridge World* magazine, wrote an excellent article some time ago about defending against difficult conventions, and he proposed the following thesis (paraphrased here): because the convention is going to hurt you on some hands, you must hurt them back.

The **Best Defense to Multi** has this in mind. Double Two Diamonds to say you also have a major, only your hand is better! If it happens to be the same major as the one on your right, you may very well be in luck — at least you didn't overcall in the suit. After you double, either you or partner may have a chance later to double responsively, showing the other major.

Notice that we double with a major, which leaves two hearts and two spades available for strong overcalls showing clubs and diamonds respectively. This is a great advantage over having to overcall at the three-level, where investigation is very clumsy. This also allows the three-of-a minor overcall to be weaker, another counter-attacking tool against the Multi. Because third hand (your LHO) does not know which major his partner has (the Achilles heel of Multi in competition), your three-club or three-diamond overcall might win an easy 10 IMPs or achieve a top at matchpoints.

If you have a takeout double of one of the majors, you pass two diamonds and later double, when they bid your short suit.

If you pass two diamonds and partner bids in fourth chair over responder's two-heart or two-spade response, it is natural; double by him is takeout.

Both vul.

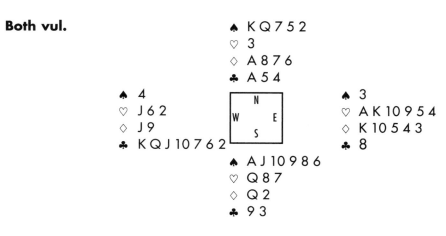

```
                        ♠ K Q 7 5 2
                        ♡ 3
                        ◇ A 8 7 6
                        ♣ A 5 4
        ♠ 4                              ♠ 3
        ♡ J 6 2              N           ♡ A K 10 9 5 4
        ◇ J 9          W         E       ◇ K 10 5 4 3
        ♣ K Q J 10 7 6 2         S       ♣ 8
                        ♠ A J 10 9 8 6
                        ♡ Q 8 7
                        ◇ Q 2
                        ♣ 9 3
```

West	North	East	South
			2◇
3♣	all pass		

West's three-clubs steals the pot, because North is confident that his partner holds a weak two-bid in hearts. West scores +130, when North-South can score +650, by taking eleven tricks in spades. The sacrifice in hearts is way too expensive, and in any case, isn't a plus score better than a minus?

DEFENSIVE AND CARDPLAY CONVENTIONS

PART THREE

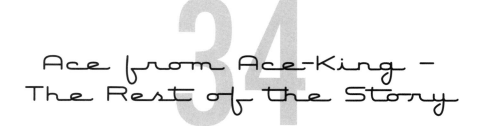

Ace from Ace-King – The Rest of the Story

The modern style of opening leads against suit contracts is as follows:

From A-K-x lead the ace; from K-Q-x lead the king.

However, there are exceptions with which you need to be familiar. You should lead the king from ace-king when:

1. **You hold A-K doubleton;**

2. **You are leading against a contract at the five-level or higher;**

3. **You are leading partner's bid suit.**

Once we have stopped leading the dreaded unsupported ace, we can use the lead of the ace to (usually) show the king.

The old-fashioned ambiguous lead of the king from ace-king or king-queen gives the defense a signaling headache when third hand holds the jack.

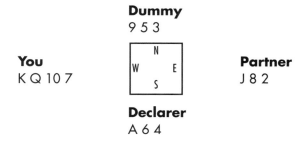

```
                    Dummy
                    9 5 3
                    ┌─────────┐
        You         │    N    │      Partner
       K Q 10 7     │ W     E │      J 8 2
                    │    S    │
                    └─────────┘
                    Declarer
                    A 6 4
```

If you are leading from the king-queen, partner wants to encourage you to continue when he holds the jack.

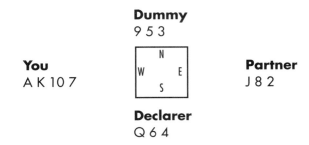

Dummy
9 5 3

You
A K 10 7

N
W   E
S

Partner
J 8 2

Declarer
Q 6 4

If you are leading from the ace-king, partner wants to discourage a continuation.

Another scenario is the 'Bath Coup'. Suppose the contract is four spades and you lead the king of hearts as West:

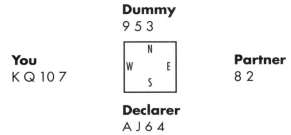

Dummy
9 5 3

You
K Q 10 7

N
W   E
S

Partner
8 2

Declarer
A J 6 4

If your king lead is ambiguous, partner doesn't know whether to play the 8 or the 2. If you hold the ace-king, he wants you to continue for a ruff. But if he plays the 8 on the actual layout, declarer will duck and you will next lead into declarer's A-J.

Leading the ace from ace-king eliminates these uncomfortable situations. In the first hand on p. 143, you lead the king and partner signals encouragement. In the second situation, you lead the ace and partner makes a discouraging signal. In the third diagram, you lead the king and partner again plays the deuce to discourage.

If you hold the ace-king doubleton, you lead the king and next the ace. Partner will understand that this is a doubleton, since you have led in your honors in reverse order. When you lead the king, he signals attitude, assuming you hold the king-queen. But when he sees the ace next, he should give you a suit-preference signal, indicating where his entry lies:

Defensive and Cardplay Conventions

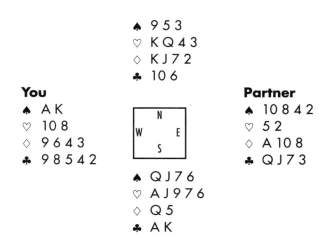

Against four hearts, you lead the king of spades and partner denies the jack by signaling with the two. When you next play the ace of spades, partner realizes that you are leading from the ace-king doubleton and gives you a suit-preference signal, the ten of spades, for the higher-ranking suit. This indicates a diamond entry. You shift to a diamond and partner returns a spade for you to ruff, setting the contract by one trick.

There are three other situations where the lead of an ace does not promise the king, and these are the situations where you might lead an unsupported ace against a suit contract:

1. **You hold the singleton ace ;**

2. **You are on lead against a contract at the five-level or higher;**

3. **You hold an unsupported ace in partner's bid suit.**

Against a high-level contract it is often important to cash your tricks quickly, setting the contract. If you don't cash the tricks on opening lead, you may lose them:

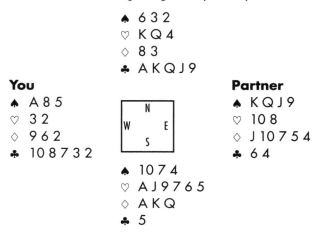

West	North	East	South
			1♡
pass	3♣	pass	3♢
pass	4♡	pass	5♡
all pass			

Declarer's five-heart bid was a slam try, denying a spade control by his failure to cuebid four spades. North didn't have the spade control either, so he passed. Through their scientific bidding, the opponents have told you they don't have a spade control. (Thank you very much!) If you don't lead your unsupported ace here, declarer will discard all of his spades on dummy's clubs and make seven.

When holding an unsupported ace in partner's suit, it is often a good idea not to lead it. However, if you have nothing better to do, you may lead the ace:

Hand A
♠ 7 6 3
♡ A 2
♢ Q J 10 4
♣ 9 8 5 3

Hand B
♠ 7 6 3
♡ A 2
♢ Q 9 4 2
♣ 9 8 5 3

You	North	Partner	South
pass	1♣	1♡	1♠
pass	2♠	pass	3♠
all pass			

On Hand A you have an attractive diamond lead despite the fact that partner overcalled in hearts. On Hand B there is no reason to lead anything other than a heart.

In these two situations where the lead of the ace does not promise the king, we revert to the king lead from either ace-king or king-queen. Partner will signal attitude, assuming you have led from the king-queen (the more likely scenario).

Here's a cute hand from real life. East and West had not discussed 'the rest of the story' of ace from ace-king leads.

E-W vul.

Dummy
♠ 10 7 4
♡ Q J
♢ K J 8 7 6
♣ K 10 9

```
     N
  W     E
     S
```

You
♠ Q J 6
♡ 10 9 7 5 4
♢ 9 4
♣ Q 8 2

West	North	East	South
			1◇
pass	3◇	pass	3♡
pass	4◇	pass	5♣
pass	5◇	all pass	

The opening lead is the ♠A. So what card do you play at Trick 1?
The whole layout was:

Dummy
♠ 10 7 4
♡ Q J
◇ K J 8 7 6
♣ K 10 9

♠ A 8 3 2
♡ K 6 3 2
◇ —
♣ J 7 6 5 4

You
♠ Q J 6
♡ 10 9 7 5 4
◇ 9 4
♣ Q 8 2

♠ K 9 5
♡ A 8
◇ A Q 10 5 3 2
♣ A 3

Partner found the winning lead. A heart or club lead would have given away the contract. If partner doesn't panic on your play of the ♠6 (by switching to another suit), but continues spades, the contract will be set. In real life, though, East played the queen under the ace, the correct play if West's lead showed the ace-king. Uh-oh!

Ten Promises, Jack Denies

Ten promises, Jack denies is a lead convention used against notrump contracts. The ten promises the jack or nine, plus the ace, king or queen. The jack denies a higher honor.

> From A J 10 3 2, lead the ten.
> From K J 10 3 2, lead the ten.
> From K 10 9 3 2, lead the ten.
> From Q 10 9 3 2, lead the ten.
> From J 10 8 3 2, lead the jack.
> From 10 9 7 4 2, lead the nine (or low).

The advantage of this convention is that it saves partner guesswork when he gains the lead and must decide whether to continue your suit:

Both vul.

	♠ 8 7 4	
	♡ K Q J 10 2	
	◇ 7 2	
	♣ Q 7 2	

♠ K J 10 3 2		♠ Q 9 5
♡ 7 6 3	N	♡ A 9 4
◇ 8 6 3	W E	◇ Q J 10 9
♣ 5 4	S	♣ 8 6 3

	♠ A 6	
	♡ 8 5	
	◇ A K 5 4	
	♣ A K J 10 9	

West	North	East	South
			1♣
pass	1♡	pass	2NT
pass	3NT	all pass	

West led the jack of spades. East signaled with the nine and declarer took the ace. Declarer played a heart to dummy, which East won. But East wasn't sure whether to play back a spade or shift to a diamond! What if the deal was:

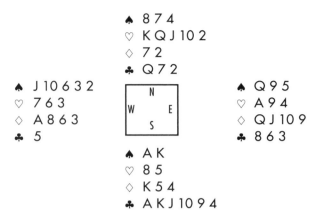

```
                    ♠ 8 7 4
                    ♡ K Q J 10 2
                    ◇ 7 2
                    ♣ Q 7 2
  ♠ J 10 6 3 2        N          ♠ Q 9 5
  ♡ 7 6 3                        ♡ A 9 4
  ◇ A 8 6 3      W       E       ◇ Q J 10 9
  ♣ 5                S           ♣ 8 6 3
                    ♠ A K
                    ♡ 8 5
                    ◇ K 5 4
                    ♣ A K J 10 9 4
```

West's card is usually a count card in this situation. East cannot duck his ace of hearts and await a clarifying signal from West because in both cases the king of hearts is declarer's ninth trick! What should East do — continue spades or switch to diamonds? It's a guess.

Playing ten promises and jack denies, East has an easy time. When West leads the *ten* of spades, East later wins the ace of hearts and returns a spade. When West leads the *jack* of spades, East wins the ace of hearts and returns a diamond. Easy-shmeezy.

SO WHY DOESN'T EVERYONE PLAY THIS WAY?

The drawback is that declarer becomes privy to some useful information:

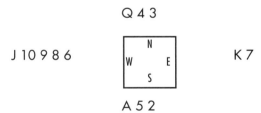

```
              Q 4 3
                 N
J 10 9 8 6    W     E    K 7
                 S
              A 5 2
```

South is delighted to know when West leads the jack that East holds the king, because he can play the suit as if he is looking at all the cards. Sometimes he catches the doubleton king (above), and at other times he knows to block the suit for the defense:

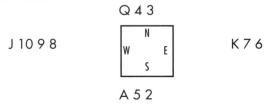

```
              Q 4 3
                 N
J 10 9 8      W     E    K 7 6
                 S
              A 5 2
```

South wins the first trick with the ace. West regains the lead and continues his suit, but South refuses to put up the queen. The defense can take two tricks, but not three.

One idea is to falsecard when you are sure your partner cannot be led astray. For example, suppose the bidding goes 1NT-3NT and you're on lead with:

♠ K J 10 9 4   ♡ A 8 4   ◇ K 9 7   ♣ J 3

You know that if partner gains the lead, he is unlikely to have anything better to do than return your suit (since the card he gains the lead with is probably his only honor). So lead the jack! The whole deal could be:

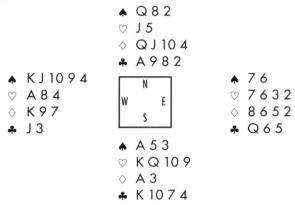

```
                  ♠ Q 8 2
                  ♡ J 5
                  ◇ Q J 10 4
                  ♣ A 9 8 2
  ♠ K J 10 9 4        N           ♠ 7 6
  ♡ A 8 4        W         E      ♡ 7 6 3 2
  ◇ K 9 7             S           ◇ 8 6 5 2
  ♣ J 3                           ♣ Q 6 5
                  ♠ A 5 3
                  ♡ K Q 10 9
                  ◇ A 3
                  ♣ K 10 7 4
```

If you lead the honest ten, declarer can win the queen, lose a heart to you, win the third round of spades with his ace, and duck a club into the East hand. East shifts to a diamond, but declarer wins, taking two spades, three hearts, one diamond and three clubs in all.

If you lead the tricky jack, denying a higher honor, declarer wins the ace, knocks out your ace of hearts, and ducks the ten of spades when you play it! Now you merrily cash your spades for down one.

Lead-Directing Doubles Against Notrump Contracts

36

PREVIEW

Doubles are used for a great many things in modern bridge – sometimes even for penalties! Do you and your partner have firm agreements on what the double means in each of the following situations?

Auction 1

Oppt	You	Oppt	Partner
1♣	pass	1NT	pass
pass	dbl		

Auction 2

Oppt	You	Oppt	Partner
1NT	pass	3NT	dbl

Auction 3

Oppt	You	Oppt	Partner
1♡	pass	1♠	pass
1NT	pass	4NT	pass
6NT	pass	pass	dbl

Auction 4

Oppt	You	Oppt	Partner
1NT	pass	2♣	pass
2♠	pass	3NT	dbl

Auction 1

Oppt	You	Oppt	Partner
1♣	pass	1NT	pass
pass	dbl		

This double shows a good hand with a 'stack' in dummy's bid suit. That's true of any such auction:

Oppt	You	Oppt	Partner
1 suit	pass	1NT	pass
pass	dbl		

This is also known as a Trap Pass(see page 191).

Auction 2

Oppt	You	Oppt	Partner
1NT	pass	3NT	dbl

Many people play that this double calls for a spade lead. Others play that it means, 'Partner, please lead your weaker major.'

Auction 3

Oppt	You	Oppt	Partner
1♡	pass	1♠	pass
1NT	pass	4NT	pass
6NT	pass	pass	dbl

In standard practice, partner's double is a **Lightner double** and calls for the lead of dummy's suit. More often, however, it is the lead of an unbid suit that will defeat the contract rather than the lead of dummy's suit. But which of the two unbid suits? Double asks for the higher-ranking unbid suit. Therefore, if partner doesn't double, when in doubt the opening leader leads the lower-ranking unbid suit.

Defensive and Cardplay Conventions

Here's a full-deal example:

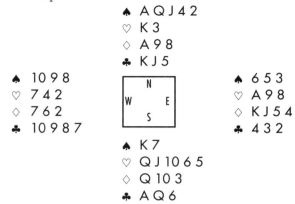

```
              ♠ A Q J 4 2
              ♡ K 3
              ◇ A 9 8
              ♣ K J 5

♠ 10 9 8            N            ♠ 6 5 3
♡ 7 4 2        W         E       ♡ A 9 8
◇ 7 6 2                          ◇ K J 5 4
♣ 10 9 8 7          S            ♣ 4 3 2

              ♠ K 7
              ♡ Q J 10 6 5
              ◇ Q 10 3
              ♣ A Q 6
```

West	North	East	South
			1♡
pass	1♠	pass	1NT
pass	4NT	pass	6NT
pass	pass	dbl	

East doubles, asking for the higher-ranking of the unbid suits. If the ace or queen of diamonds is in dummy, a diamond lead will defeat the slam. After the normal club lead, six notrump is cold.

Auction 4

Oppt	You	Oppt	Partner
1NT	pass	2♣	pass
2♠	pass	3NT	dbl

The double here calls for dummy's real suit, which is hearts. What if the two-club bid doesn't promise hearts? Perhaps it's the only way responder can invite to 3NT, for example, in this auction:

Oppt	You	Oppt	Partner
1NT	pass	2♣	pass
2♠	pass	2NT	pass
3NT	pass	pass	dbl

The double nevertheless calls for a heart lead. It's best to play that if you want a club lead, you have to double Stayman (you can't wait and double 3NT later).

Again, a full-deal example:

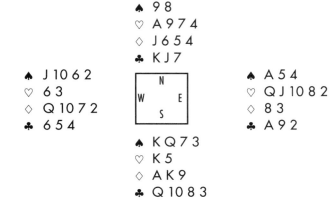

```
               ♠ 9 8
               ♡ A 9 7 4
               ◇ J 6 5 4
               ♣ K J 7
♠ J 10 6 2                      ♠ A 5 4
♡ 6 3           N               ♡ Q J 10 8 2
◇ Q 10 7 2    W   E             ◇ 8 3
♣ 6 5 4         S               ♣ A 9 2
               ♠ K Q 7 3
               ♡ K 5
               ◇ A K 9
               ♣ Q 10 8 3
```

West	North	East	South
			1NT
pass	2♣	pass	2♠
pass	2NT	pass	3NT
pass	pass	dbl	all pass

After a spade or diamond lead, declarer has an easy time coming to nine tricks. After a heart lead, his contract is doomed.

The Slam Spade Double

37

Sam Spade was a fictional detective from San Francisco who was featured in *The Maltese Falcon* and other Dashiell Hammett books and films. But the **Slam Spade Double** comes from a game played at the old Mayfair Club in New York City called 'cut-throat' or 'goulie' (short for 'goulash'). In this game, hands would be redealt from a passed-out deal without being shuffled! Wild distributions were the result, and every once in a while, fantastic slams or grand slams were reached, with each side owning two-suit fits. If you got off to the wrong lead against one of these slams, you could easily lose a fast hundred dollars. One way of getting the lead right against these goulie slams was for the fourth seat to double only when he wanted a spade lead (or a heart lead when spades were trumps). The failure to double also had a meaning — don't lead a spade.

The Slam Spade Double can be used in regular bridge as well. Big rewards come when the bidding goes 1NT-6NT and you hold the ace-king of spades behind dummy and can double for a spade lead. This is admittedly rare, but it also covers the more common Keycard Blackwood mix-ups and similar errors, where seven is reached off an ace. When the opening leader's partner holds the ace, it can be frustrating. But if you can double to say, 'Lead the highest-ranking unbid suit,' you have a better shot at defeating the grand slam.

Both vul.

```
                        ♠ 4 2
                        ♡ A Q J 7 6
                        ◇ A Q 8 3
                        ♣ 9 7
     ♠ Q 10 8 7 3         ┌─────────┐         ♠ A J 9 5
     ♡ 5 3 2              │    N    │         ♡ 10 9 8
     ◇ J 10 6 4          │ W     E │         ◇ K 7 5 2
     ♣ 6                  │    S    │         ♣ 3 2
                         └─────────┘
                        ♠ K 6
                        ♡ K 4
                        ◇ 9
                        ♣ A K Q J 10 8 5 4
```

West	North	East	South
	1♡	pass	4NT[1]
pass	5♠[2]	pass	7NT[3]
pass	pass	dbl![4]	

1. He means it as regular Blackwood.
2. He answers Keycard Blackwood for hearts (5♠ = two with the queen).
3. He thinks his partner has three aces and can count thirteen tricks.
4. Lead a spade, partner!

Notice that if West leads any suit but spades, declarer has fourteen tricks!

This next example (from real life — the U.S. Bermuda Bowl Trials) is more inferential and therefore more difficult. You, West, hold:

North-South vul.

♠ 9 7 4 2   ♡ —   ◇ 9 7 6 4 3 2   ♣ 7 6 5

West	North	East	South
pass	1♠	pass	2♡
pass	5NT[1]	pass	6NT[2]
pass	7♡	all pass	

1. Grand slam force.
2. Two of the top three heart honors.

Playing Slam Spade Doubles, what do you lead and why?

They bid spades and hearts, so double from partner calls for a diamond lead (the higher-ranking unbid suit). Partner didn't double, so a diamond lead is out. That narrows the choice down to a spade lead vs. a club lead. Which is more likely:

a) North bid 5NT with a club loser; or
b) North bid 5NT with long solid spades, a big heart fit, and first-round controls in both minors?

Obviously the answer is (b). Therefore, you lead a spade and hope for the best. The whole hand was:

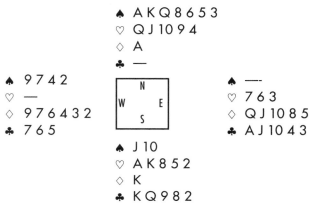

```
                    ♠ A K Q 8 6 5 3
                    ♡ Q J 10 9 4
                    ◇ A
                    ♣ —
   ♠ 9 7 4 2              N              ♠ —
   ♡ —              W           E        ♡ 7 6 3
   ◇ 9 7 6 4 3 2          S              ◇ Q J 10 8 5
   ♣ 7 6 5                                ♣ A J 10 4 3
                    ♠ J 10
                    ♡ A K 8 5 2
                    ◇ K
                    ♣ K Q 9 8 2
```

West	North	East	South
pass	1♠	pass	2♡
pass	5NT	pass	6NT
pass	7♡	all pass	

You may look at this deal and say, 'Yes, but I play Lightner Doubles, so my partner could double for a spade lead here anyway and get his ruff.' When there are two unbid suits, you cannot play both the Slam Spade Double and Lightner Doubles (the Lightner Double means: 'Lead dummy's first-bid suit' and the Slam Spade Double means: 'Lead the higher-ranking unbid suit' — obviously, the double must mean one thing or the other). In the long run, the Slam Spade Doubles come up more frequently, because you are more likely to need the lead of an unbid suit than a bid suit to defeat a slam or grand slam, unless you are void in the first suit bid by dummy (in which case, a Lightner Double may cause them to run to notrump anyway).

On the above hand, the Lightner Double works as well (because East is on lead should they run to 7NT), but it wouldn't work so well if we exchange East's club ace with South's club king:

```
                    ♠ A K Q 8 6 5 3
                    ♡ Q J 10 9 4
                    ◊ A
                    ♣ —
    ♠ 9 7 4 2          ┌─────┐          ♠ —
    ♡ —                │  N  │          ♡ 7 6 3
    ◊ 9 7 6 4 3 2      │W   E│          ◊ Q J 10 8 5
    ♣ 7 6 5            │  S  │          ♣ K J 10 4 3
                       └─────┘
                    ♠ J 10
                    ♡ A K 8 5 2
                    ◊ K
                    ♣ A Q 9 8 2
```

West	North	East	South
pass	1♠	pass	2♡
pass	5NT	pass	6NT
pass	7♡	dbl[1]	pass
pass	7♠	pass	pass
dbl[2]	pass	pass	7NT
all pass			

1. Lightner Double – 'Please lead dummy's first-bid suit (a spade).'
2. Lightner Double – 'Please lead dummy's first-bid suit (a heart).'

TELLING THE DIFFERENCE

What does this double mean?

West	North	East	South
			1♠
pass	2◊	pass	2♡
pass	3♠	pass	4♠
pass	4NT	pass	5◊
pass	6♠	dbl	

This time it's a Lightner Double because there is only one unbid suit. The Slam Spade Double operates only when there are two or three (or even four!) unbid suits.

If there are three unbid suits, the double calls for the highest-ranking suit:

West	North	East	South
			1♡
pass	4NT	pass	5♡
pass	6♡	?	

Now double would say, 'Please lead a spade,' and pass would say, 'Please lead a club or a diamond.' At least here, at worst West makes his best guess between two suits rather than three. If there are four unbid suits (1NT-6NT), double calls for a spade.

What if they bid two suits and your side has bid one suit?

West	North	East	South
		pass	1NT
2♡	2NT[1]	4♡	pass
pass	4NT[1]	pass	5♣
pass	pass	5♡	pass
pass	6♣	dbl	all pass

1. Minors.

North showed both minor suits. East's double is a Slam Spade Double, asking West to lead the higher of the two unbid (by them) suits! Another success, as this was the whole deal:

Both vul.

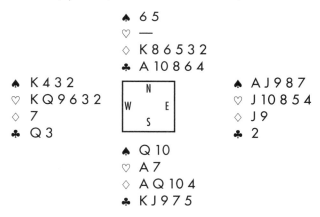

```
                  ♠ 6 5
                  ♡ —
                  ◇ K 8 6 5 3 2
                  ♣ A 10 8 6 4
♠ K 4 3 2                          ♠ A J 9 8 7
♡ K Q 9 6 3 2        N             ♡ J 10 8 5 4
◇ 7              W       E         ◇ J 9
♣ Q 3                S             ♣ 2
                  ♠ Q 10
                  ♡ A 7
                  ◇ A Q 10 4
                  ♣ K J 9 7 5
```

The Lead-Directing Pass

In today's game, where it seems that almost every auction is competitive, it's important to realize that you have options available to you that don't exist without the opponents' bidding. One such option is the **Lead-Directing Pass**. Have you been in the position where you wanted to double a cuebid but were reluctant to give the opponents extra chances to show their cards? After you double, passes and redoubles by the opponents convey information without using up any space! The solution is to reverse the meanings of pass and double. Using this agreement, if a suit has been bid by your side and the opponents cuebid this suit, double says, 'Don't lead it' and pass says, 'Lead it!' This is simply the reverse of the traditional lead-directing double. It is a very powerful weapon against cuebids. Obviously, you can't double cuebids with two little cards in the suit, because one day someone will redouble and make three overtricks. So this system applies only when your side has shown length in the suit that has been cuebid.

Most of the time you want the lead in the suit that you have bid, and the pass is used to get that lead while presenting the opponents no extra bidding space. For example:

You	LHO	Partner	RHO
1♡	1♠	pass	2♡
pass			

Pass says, 'Lead a heart.' Notice if you double two hearts, you give LHO two extra calls, pass or redouble, to define his overcall further. Therefore, you want to double as infrequently as possible, and since you usually want the lead of the suit you have bid, you will be passing the cuebid often.

Here's an example from world championship play (in 1993, U.S.A. vs. Germany). East (Kerri Sanborn) and West (Karen McCallum) were using the Lead-Directing Pass.

Neither vul.

```
                    ♠ K 10 7 6
                    ♡ K 9 8 5 3
                    ◇ K 8 4
                    ♣ 4
  ♠ 9 3 2                              ♠ Q
  ♡ 7 6          ┌──────────┐          ♡ A Q J 10
  ◇ Q 9 7 3      │    N     │          ◇ J 10 6 5 2
  ♣ A Q 7 3      │  W     E │          ♣ 8 6 5
                 │    S     │
                 └──────────┘
                    ♠ A J 8 5 4
                    ♡ 4 2
                    ◇ A
                    ♣ K J 10 9 2
```

West	North	East	South
	pass	2◇[1]	2♠
3◇	4◇	dbl[2]	redbl
pass	4♡	dbl[3]	4♠
all pass			

1. A loose weak two-bid in diamonds (conventionally known as a McCallum Two-Bid).
2. Don't lead diamonds!
3. Lead hearts.

When North chose to cuebid with her hand, she gave Kerri Sanborn the chance to make a Don't Lead My Suit Double (i.e., the flip side of the Lead-Directing Pass). South redoubled, which was of less value than it would have been over a standard Lead-Directing Double, because it only confirmed what East had already said, a diamond lead was not good for the defense. Now North had the 'golden opportunity' to make a second cuebid, albeit a questionable one, in hearts, and Kerri was back in action with a standard Lead-Directing Double (since East-West had never bid hearts).

Karen McCallum led a heart against four spades and Kerri won and shifted to a club. West won and played a second heart to Kerri, who then played a third heart. It was now quite reasonable for the declarer to ruff high with the ace of spades and finesse West for the queen. When this lost, the contract was down one.

Using standard Lead-Directing Doubles, East passes North's 4◇ cuebid and South bids 4♠, ending the auction. West might find the heart lead anyway, but she really has no reason to open up the heart suit so a diamond lead is more normal.

Almost everyone plays 'queen demands the jack' on opening leads against notrump contracts. This simplifies the defense for hands like:

Dummy
3 2

You
K Q 10 9

```
    N
W       E
    S
```

Partner
8 7 6 5

Declarer
A J 4

You lead the queen instead of the king, and when partner fails to follow with the jack, you know he doesn't have it. This saves you from a Bath Coup (in declarer ducks), or from setting up declarer's jack later in the play (in the event declarer wins the first trick).

If partner doesn't have the jack, which card should he play? Count? Attitude? And to make life even more complicated, what if your queen-lead was *not* from KQ109x, but rather it was a 'regular' queen-lead from the queen-jack?

Situation 1

	Dummy	
	3 2	

You		**Partner**
Q J 9 8 6	[N W E S]	10 7 5 (or) 7 5 4

Declarer
A K 4 (or) A K 10

or

Situation #2

	Dummy	
	3 2	

You		**Partner**
Q J 9 8 6	[N W E S]	7 5

Declarer
A K 10 4

In Situation #1, you'd like to know about that ten. If partner plays low, giving count, and declarer wins the king, you might gain the lead and have no idea whether to continue your suit. Did declarer begin with AKx or AK10?

In Situation #2, if partner plays high (count), when you regain the lead you don't know if partner has 10xxx or xx!

THE SOLUTION

Drop the Touching Honor

With this agreement, then the lead of an

> **Ace demands the king**
> **King demands the queen**
> **Queen demands the jack**
> **Jack demands the ten**

The ace is led from A-K-x-x, the king is led from A-K-J-10.
The king is led from K-Q-x-x, the queen is led from K-Q-10-9.
The queen is led from Q-J-x-x, the jack is led from Q-J-9-8.

When partner holds the honor that opening leader is supposed to hold, he drops it. Otherwise, he gives attitude.

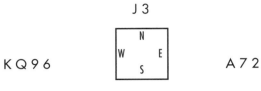

```
              J 3
            ┌─────┐
            │  N  │
   K Q 9 6  │W   E│   A 7 2
            │  S  │
            └─────┘
            10 8 5 4
```

West leads the king and East plays the seven, attitude.

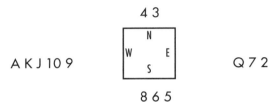

```
              4 3
            ┌─────┐
            │  N  │
  A K J 10 9│W   E│   Q 7 2
            │  S  │
            └─────┘
             8 6 5
```

West leads the king and East drops the queen.

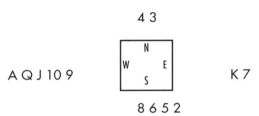

```
              4 3
            ┌─────┐
            │  N  │
  A Q J 10 9│W   E│   K 7
            │  S  │
            └─────┘
            8 6 5 2
```

West leads the ace and East drops the king.

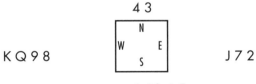

```
              4 3
            ┌─────┐
            │  N  │
   K Q 9 8  │W   E│   J 7 2
            │  S  │
            └─────┘
           A 10 6 5
```

West leads the king and East signals he has the jack (or ace) by playing the seven.

Defensive and Cardplay Conventions

Suit Preference in the Trump Suit

Most players use the trump suit only to signal extra length and/or a desire to ruff. But when declarer is obviously drawing all the trumps, there's little point in that. Instead, you could use a Trump Suit-preference Signal. Make your opponent pay for drawing trumps early by signaling where your strength is! This may easily mean the difference in defeating the contract or, at matchpoints, stopping a crucial overtrick. The way to signal is to play high-low for the highest-ranking side-suit, and low-high for the lowest.

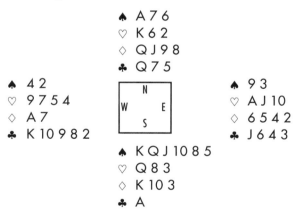

```
              ♠ A 7 6
              ♡ K 6 2
              ◇ Q J 9 8
              ♣ Q 7 5
  ♠ 4 2            N          ♠ 9 3
  ♡ 9 7 5 4                   ♡ A J 10
  ◇ A 7       W       E       ◇ 6 5 4 2
  ♣ K 10 9 8 2      S         ♣ J 6 4 3
              ♠ K Q J 10 8 5
              ♡ Q 8 3
              ◇ K 10 3
              ♣ A
```

On this deal at matchpoints, many Wests led a heart against South's four-spade contract. East put in the ten and South won the queen. South was reluctant to play on diamonds before drawing trumps, and East took full advantage by applying Suit Preference in the Trump Suit. He signaled 9-3 in spades, so when declarer attacked diamonds by playing the king, West won and knew to continue hearts, holding the contract to ten tricks.

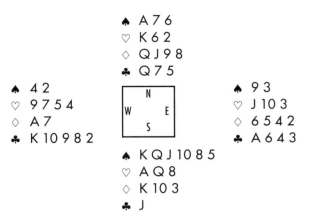

♠ A 7 6
♡ K 6 2
◇ Q J 9 8
♣ Q 7 5

♠ 4 2   ♠ 9 3
♡ 9 7 5 4   ♡ J 10 3
◇ A 7   ◇ 6 5 4 2
♣ K 10 9 8 2   ♣ A 6 4 3

♠ K Q J 10 8 5
♡ A Q 8
◇ K 10 3
♣ J

On this layout, in contrast, East follows with the 3-9 of trumps, suit preference for clubs. West shifts to a club when he wins the ◇A and holds the contract to five.

Obvious Shift Carding (Simplified)

Obvious Shift Carding is a book* all by itself, but here it is in a nutshell.

At Trick 1, the opening leader's partner gives an attitude signal which is not only about the suit led, but about another suit! Which suit? First you eliminate two suits: 1) the trump suit; and 2) the suit led.

For example:

Dummy   ♠ A 6 3 2   ♡ K 5 4   ◇ 9 7 2   ♣ 7 6 5

Declarer	**Dummy**
1♠	2♠
4♠	

Partner leads the ace of clubs. The eliminated suits are: 1) spades (the trump suit); and 2) clubs (the suit led).

Next you look at the remaining two suits. The weaker of these two suits is the 'obvious shift' suit. In this case, the two remaining suits are hearts and diamonds. Dummy's diamonds are weaker than dummy's hearts, so diamonds is the 'obvious shift' suit. In standard attitude signals, a low card means, 'I do not like the suit you led.' Usually, the opening leader will shift at Trick 2, or, if declarer wins the first trick, partner will play another suit when he regains the lead. Here, too, the low card means, 'I do not like the suit you led' but it also means 'Go ahead and make the obvious shift.' A high card means: 'I may not love the suit you led, but I want to warn you not to make the obvious shift, because I have no high honor in that suit.'

---

*   For a book-length discussion of Obvious Shift Carding, see *A Switch in Time* by Matthew & Pamela Granovetter.

Back to our example:

Dummy ♠ A 6 3 2 ♡ K 5 4 ◇ 9 7 2 ♣ 7 6 5

Declarer	**Dummy**
1♠	2♠
4♠	

The opening leader leads the ace of clubs. If the opening leader's partner plays a high club, it means 'I do not have the ace or king of diamonds' and if the opening leader's partner plays a low club, it means, 'I have the ace or king of diamonds (dummy's weaker side suit); go ahead and shift if you want to.'

This system requires that you use some judgment — for example, if you have a doubleton club and a high diamond honor, you high-low in clubs because you would like a club ruff:

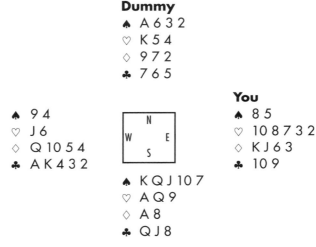

Dummy
♠ A 6 3 2
♡ K 5 4
◇ 9 7 2
♣ 7 6 5

♠ 9 4
♡ J 6
◇ Q 10 5 4
♣ A K 4 3 2

You
♠ 8 5
♡ 10 8 7 3 2
◇ K J 6 3
♣ 10 9

♠ K Q J 10 7
♡ A Q 9
◇ A 8
♣ Q J 8

If you don't get your club ruff, you are not going to defeat this contract!

If you cannot easily identify dummy's weaker suit, the lower-ranking weak suit is arbitrarily deemed to be the 'obvious shift' suit:

Dummy ♠ A K 5 ♡ 7 6 4 ◇ 8 7 2 ♣ 9 7 4 3

Declarer	**Dummy**
1♠	2♠
4♠	

Partner leads a high club. Dummy's hearts and diamonds are identical, so diamonds is the obvious shift suit, because it's lower-ranking.

Here's an example from real life of how Obvious Shift works:

Both vul.

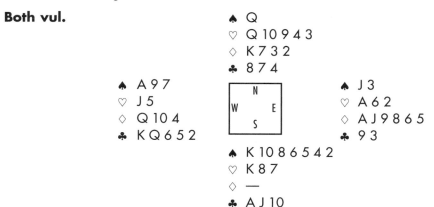

```
                    ♠ Q
                    ♡ Q 10 9 4 3
                    ◇ K 7 3 2
                    ♣ 8 7 4
    ♠ A 9 7              N           ♠ J 3
    ♡ J 5          W         E       ♡ A 6 2
    ◇ Q 10 4            S           ◇ A J 9 8 6 5
    ♣ K Q 6 5 2                     ♣ 9 3
                    ♠ K 10 8 6 5 4 2
                    ♡ K 8 7
                    ◇ —
                    ♣ A J 10
```

East-West bid diamonds and the Australian South got to four spades. West led the queen of diamonds, dummy played low, and East played the nine. South ruffed and played a spade to the queen, a heart to his king, and the king of spades, squashing East's jack. So far so good, from declarer's point of view, but he appears to have four losers nonetheless: one spade, one heart and two clubs. So how did he make +620 to win 9 IMPs?

When West won the ace of trumps, he wasn't sure what to do. If we switch East's ace of hearts with South's ace of clubs, West must switch to a low club so that the defense can take three club tricks before declarer's club losers go away on the hearts. This is what West played for. He played a low club and the contract rolled home. How does West know to avoid the deadly club shift? Obvious shift players don't even have to think about this one! East's nine of diamonds play at Trick 1 denies tolerance for the 'obvious shift suit', which is dummy's weak suit — clubs. If East holds the ace of clubs instead of the ace of hearts, he plays the five of diamonds at Trick 1. Remember, the signal is not only about the suit led, it is about the obvious shift suit. If you can't stand the obvious shift, then of course you want partner to continue with the suit he led and not shift, so you play an encouraging card.

What happens when you want partner to shift, but not to the 'obvious shift' suit? In some circumstances, you can ask for the fourth suit (i.e., not the suit led, trumps, or dummy's weaker side suit) by playing an unusual card. Let's change the above example slightly:

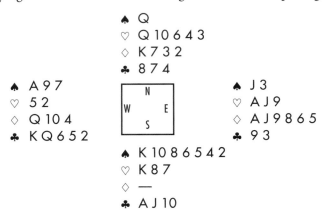

♠ Q
♥ Q 10 6 4 3
♦ K 7 3 2
♣ 8 7 4

♠ A 9 7
♥ 5 2
♦ Q 10 4
♣ K Q 6 5 2

♠ J 3
♥ A J 9
♦ A J 9 8 6 5
♣ 9 3

♠ K 10 8 6 5 4 2
♥ K 8 7
♦ —
♣ A J 10

West leads the queen of diamonds at Trick 1 and East plays the jack. This means, 'I like dummy's strong(er) side suit; the suit you would never normally play.'

Here's another example:

North-South vul.

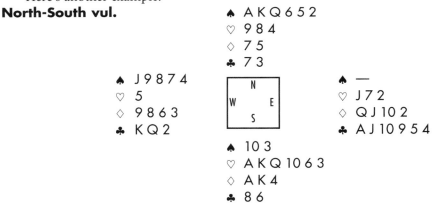

♠ A K Q 6 5 2
♥ 9 8 4
♦ 7 5
♣ 7 3

♠ J 9 8 7 4
♥ 5
♦ 9 8 6 3
♣ K Q 2

♠ —
♥ J 7 2
♦ Q J 10 2
♣ A J 10 9 5 4

♠ 10 3
♥ A K Q 10 6 3
♦ A K 4
♣ 8 6

West	North	East	South
		3♣	3♥
4♣	4♥	all pass	

West leads the king of clubs, and East follows with the jack. This is an unusual card asking for an unusual shift. At Trick 2, West leads his smallest spade (suit preference) for East to ruff, and East returns a low club to West's queen for a second ruff to set the contract.

If East has a spade, he follows to the first club with the nine, which means 'continue clubs, don't shift to diamonds':

```
                    ♠ A K Q 6 5 2
                    ♡ 9 8 4
                    ◇ 7 5
                    ♣ 7 3
    ♠ J 9 8 7                          ♠ 4
    ♡ 5 2           ┌──────────┐       ♡ J 7
    ◇ A 9 8 6       │    N     │       ◇ Q J 10 2
    ♣ K Q 2         │  W    E  │       ♣ A J 10 9 5 4
                    │    S     │
                    └──────────┘
                    ♠ 10 3
                    ♡ A K Q 10 6 3
                    ◇ K 4 3
                    ♣ 8 6
```

West	North	East	South
		3♣	3♡
4♣	4♡	all pass	

This time, East plays the nine on West's lead of the club king. West continues with a club to East's ace, and East switches to the queen of diamonds.

Smith Echo

The **Smith Echo** is a popular defensive signal against notrump contracts that allows one partner to tell the other whether he likes the suit that was led. After declarer wins his first trick, he will usually play his own long suit. At each defender's first opportunity, the defender signals while following suit — high-low means he likes the opening lead (Smith Echo), and low-high means he doesn't like it.

Dummy		*or*		**Dummy**
♠ 8 7				♠ 8 7

West		**East**	**West**		**East**
♠ A 10 6 4 2		♠ Q J 3	♠ A 10 6 4 2		♠ J 9 3

Declarer		**Declarer**
♠ K 9 5		♠ K Q 5

West leads his fourth-best spade against 3NT, to East's jack and declarer's king. West would like to know if East has the queen-jack or just the jack. East will tell him by playing high-low or low-high when following suit to the next suit played!

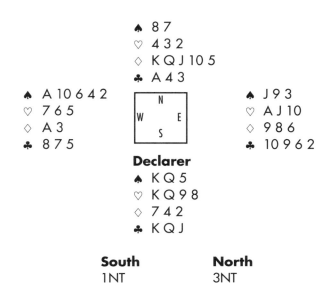

♠ 8 7
♡ 4 3 2
◇ K Q J 10 5
♣ A 4 3

♠ A 10 6 4 2   N   ♠ J 9 3
♡ 7 6 5   W   E   ♡ A J 10
◇ A 3   S   ◇ 9 8 6
♣ 8 7 5   ♣ 10 9 6 2

Declarer
♠ K Q 5
♡ K Q 9 8
◇ 7 4 2
♣ K Q J

South	North
1NT	3NT

West leads a low spade to the jack and king. West wins the second diamond and needs to know whether to continue spades or not. In this case, East followed to the diamonds up-the-line and this denies any further interest in the spade suit. West knows declarer has the queen of spades so he shifts to a heart or club.

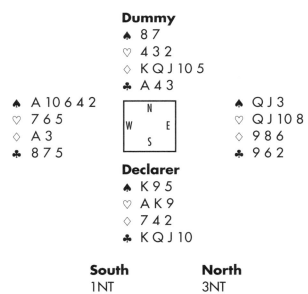

Dummy
♠ 8 7
♡ 4 3 2
◇ K Q J 10 5
♣ A 4 3

♠ A 10 6 4 2   N   ♠ Q J 3
♡ 7 6 5   W   E   ♡ Q J 10 8
◇ A 3   S   ◇ 9 8 6
♣ 8 7 5   ♣ 9 6 2

Declarer
♠ K 9 5
♡ A K 9
◇ 7 4 2
♣ K Q J 10

South	North
1NT	3NT

Again West leads a low spade to the jack and king. West wins the second diamond, noting that his partner played high-low (the Smith Echo) in diamonds. This shows the queen of spades, so West continues spades and the defense takes four spades and one diamond.

Bridge Conventions in Depth

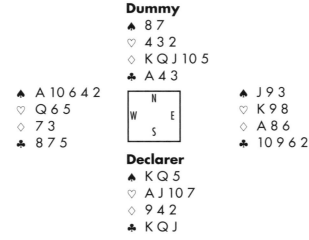

Dummy
- ♠ 8 7
- ♡ 4 3 2
- ◇ K Q J 10 5
- ♣ A 4 3

West
- ♠ A 10 6 4 2
- ♡ Q 6 5
- ◇ 7 3
- ♣ 8 7 5

East
- ♠ J 9 3
- ♡ K 9 8
- ◇ A 8 6
- ♣ 10 9 6 2

Declarer
- ♠ K Q 5
- ♡ A J 10 7
- ◇ 9 4 2
- ♣ K Q J

South	North
1NT	3NT

This time, it is West's signal that is crucial. When in with the ace of diamonds, East needs to know whether to play back a spade or switch to hearts. West's high-low in diamonds tells East, 'I like the suit I led.'

To be more precise, the high-low means, 'I prefer the suit I led to a shift to another suit.' In most cases, it also means, 'I am ready to run the suit.' Look at the next example:

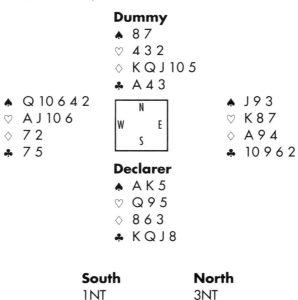

Dummy
- ♠ 8 7
- ♡ 4 3 2
- ◇ K Q J 10 5
- ♣ A 4 3

West
- ♠ Q 10 6 4 2
- ♡ A J 10 6
- ◇ 7 2
- ♣ 7 5

East
- ♠ J 9 3
- ♡ K 8 7
- ◇ A 9 4
- ♣ 10 9 6 2

Declarer
- ♠ A K 5
- ♡ Q 9 5
- ◇ 8 6 3
- ♣ K Q J 8

South	North
1NT	3NT

This time West follows low-high in diamonds, because he's not ready to run the spade suit. The low-high suggests a heart shift, if partner thinks it's necessary to cash out. East, knowing that his partner's spade suit isn't ready to run, shifts to hearts.

Let's change the deal around a little bit more:

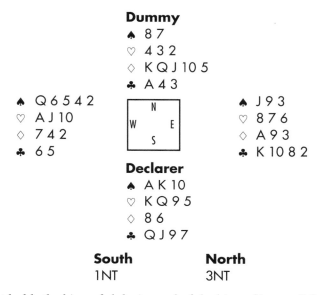

Dummy
- ♠ 8 7
- ♡ 4 3 2
- ◇ K Q J 10 5
- ♣ A 4 3

West:
- ♠ Q 6 5 4 2
- ♡ A J 10
- ◇ 7 4 2
- ♣ 6 5

East:
- ♠ J 9 3
- ♡ 8 7 6
- ◇ A 9 3
- ♣ K 10 8 2

Declarer
- ♠ A K 10
- ♡ K Q 9 5
- ◇ 8 6
- ♣ Q J 9 7

South	North
1NT	3NT

This time East holds the king of clubs instead of the king of hearts. When in with the ace of diamonds, noting West's low-high, he would continue spades anyway, knowing that the defense has time to set up spades. Don't forget: you still have to think on defense!

Some pairs play 'Reverse Smith Echo' which means they high-low when they don't like the opening-led suit – the rationale is similar to that of all the Upside-down carding agreements. However, the most sophisticated method is for the opening leader to use 'reverse' and third hand to use 'regular' Smith. The reason for playing this is a subtle one. Here is a full explanation.

If declarer leads his own suit two tricks in a row, there is no real difference between Smith Echo and Reverse Smith Echo, because you're playing the same two cards in one order or the other. Sometimes, however, a defender must win the first lead by declarer (for example, when declarer finesses into your singleton or doubleton king). On this occasion, the partner of the defender who wins the trick gets to play only one card. It's usually better to play a low card when following suit than a high one, because an unnecessarily high one may give away a trick in the suit. For example:

◇ K Q 9 8 4

◇ J 10 2   N / W E / S   ◇ A 3

◇ 7 6 5

Declarer wins the opening lead in a 3NT contract and leads a diamond at Trick 2. On the lead of the five, six or seven, second hand does not want to play the jack or ten, because it gives declarer the entire suit. If he plays the 2, declarer will probably play the king or queen and lose two tricks in the suit. So in a case like this, West does not want to give a Smith Echo, if he can help it.

Since the opening leader usually leads his best suit and usually wants that suit returned, the opening leader prefers to play Reverse Smith Echo, signaling up-the-line when he wants his suit returned, the more frequent situation. (It's less frequent that the opening leader prefers a switch to another suit.) But the opposite is true with third hand. He usually does not like the suit led, and, therefore, he would prefer to play regular Smith Echo, high-lowing also in the less frequent situations in which he likes the led suit.

Therefore, the recommended method is:

The opening leader uses Reverse Smith Echo.

Third hand uses plain Smith Echo.

FINE ARTS
CONVENTIONS

PART FOUR

Vacant Doubletons

You pick up at favorable vulnerability:

♠ 4 2   ♡ Q 6 3   ◇ A K 4 2   ♣ J 6 5 4

Partner opens 1NT (15-17). Next hand passes. What is your call?

The obvious bid is 3NT, but you're going to be a little nervous about that spade lead, aren't you? For all you know, five of a minor or even four hearts may be cold, while 3NT loses the first five spade tricks.

THE SOLUTION

The **Vacant Doubletons** convention was probably a creation of the late bridge theorist, Dave Cliff, who also invented (or was one of the first to invent) splinter bids. A vacant doubleton, or 'VD', as he used to call it, is a small doubleton, jack high at best. These little things can be a weak spot in a 3NT contract when your partner also holds a VD or even a slightly stronger double-ton.

Over the years, there have been many methods designed to pinpoint vacant doubletons after a one-notrump opening. The following is one such method, where the notrump bidder does not reveal his weakness, but instead asks responder to show his.

Let's assume the responder to 1NT has a VD, no four-card major, and enough points for game. There are two other requirements:

1.   *Responder has three to an honor in at least one major.*

2.   *Responder does not hold a six-card minor.*

How will responder tell opener about this? Much depends on your current system, but for now we'll make room for it in your 2♠ response. We'll assume you are playing transfers and you use 2♠ to show the minors. (Even if you use 2♠ for something else, you may be able to stick the VD response into your existing structure elsewhere.)

Opener	Responder
1NT	2♠[1]
2NT[2]	?

1. Either minors or a game force with a vacant doubleton.
2. Asks which type of hand.

Responder now shows his hand:

3♣	minors, forcing
3◇	vacant doubleton in clubs or diamonds
3♡	vacant doubleton in hearts
3♠	vacant doubleton in spades

After 3◇, showing a VD in either minor, opener bids 3♡ to ask which minor and responder bids 3♠ with a VD in clubs, and 3NT with a VD in diamonds.

Let's look at the preview hand again:

♠ 4 2   ♡ Q 6 3   ◇ A K 4 2   ♣ J 6 5 4

Partner opens 1NT (15-17). Next hand passes. What is your call?

Armed with your new method, you bid 2♠, showing the minors or a vacant doubleton. When partner bids 2NT, you bid 3♠, showing your VD in spades. The rest is up to partner.

Suppose partner holds this hand for his 1NT opening:

♠ A 6   ♡ A K 5 2   ◇ 7 6 3   ♣ K Q 9 2

Over 3♠, he bids 4♡ and plays the 4-3 fit. This contract has a much better chance of success than 3NT, which has almost zero play after a spade lead. Four hearts makes whenever the hearts are 3-3.

Even when partner has three spades, it may be right to play the 4-3 fit. For example, his hand could be:

♠ A 6 5   ♡ A K 10 5   ◇ 6 3   ♣ K Q 9 2

Here are some more examples:

Opener	Responder
♠ A Q J 4	♠ K 5 2
♡ J 7	♡ 4 2
◇ A Q 6	◇ K 7 5 2
♣ K 9 6 3	♣ A 7 5 4

Opener	Responder
1NT	2♠
2NT	3♡[1]
4♠	pass

1. VD in hearts.

Making ten tricks whenever spades are no worse than 4-2, as long as the clubs divide 3-2 or diamonds 3-3. Meanwhile, 3NT has zero play after a heart lead.

Opener	Responder
♠ A 10 7 5	♠ K J 2
♡ K 5 2	♡ A J 6
◇ A K 5 4	◇ Q 8 7 6 2
♣ Q 9	♣ 6 3

Opener	Responder
1NT	2♠
2NT	3◇
3♡	3♠
4♠	pass

The 3♡ bid asks which minor the VD is in, and the first step, 3♠, says it's in clubs. Four spades has some reasonable chances, while 3NT is very unlikely to make after a club lead.

OTHER APPLICATIONS

Whenever responder rebids 2NT not forcing, after using Stayman or after a transfer, opener can check back for a vacant doubleton. Here's how:

Opener	Responder
1NT	2NT
?	

Opener	Responder
1NT	2♣
2 any	2NT
?	

Opener	Responder
1NT	2◇
2♡	2NT
?	

In all cases, opener, with enough points to bid game, has the option of bidding 3♣ to ask responder if he has a vacant doubleton. Over 3♣, responder bids:

3♦	vacant doubleton in a minor suit
3♡	vacant doubleton here, if possible
3♠	vacant doubleton here, if possible
3NT	no vacant doubleton

One piece of advice: it's not useful to show a vacant doubleton in a suit shown by opener (e.g., after Stayman, if opener shows four spades, responder shouldn't bother showing a vacant doubleton in spades).

Examples:

Opener	Responder
♠ Q 4	♠ 6 3
♡ K J 10 5 4	♡ A 7 6
♦ K 3 2	♦ Q J 10 6
♣ A K 7	♣ J 6 5 4

Opener	Responder
1NT	2NT
3♣	3♠
4♡	pass

Opener has five hearts and opened 1NT to avoid rebid problems after a 1♡ opening. Over 2NT, he checks back and finds out that 4♡ is the place to be. (Yes, he could bid 3♡ over 2NT, as a natural bid, but this informs the opponents about his 5-card suit, something he would prefer to hide if 3NT becomes the final contract.)

Opener	Responder
♠ A K 6 4	♠ J 8 2
♡ A K	♡ Q J 7 5 4
♦ Q J 10 2	♦ A 4 3
♣ 9 6 2	♣ 8 3

Opener	Responder
1NT	2♦
2♡	2NT
3♣	3♦[1]
3♡	3♠[2]
4♡	pass

1. VD in clubs or diamonds.
2. VD in clubs.

Here responder transfers and rebids 2NT. Opener, who is nervous about clubs, checks if responder has a VD. When responder shows a VD in clubs or diamonds, opener bids 3♡ to ask which, and when responder shows the VD in clubs, opener tries 4♡.

Opener	Responder
♠ A Q 6	♠ K J 4 3
♡ A Q 2	♡ 10 8 7 4
◇ 3 2	◇ 6 5
♣ K Q 9 7 3	♣ A 5 2

Opener	Responder
1NT	2♣
2◇	2NT
3♣	3◇[1]
3♡	3NT[2]
4◇	4♠
pass	

1. VD in clubs or diamonds.
2. VD in diamonds.

After Stayman and 2NT, opener takes time out to check for a VD. Responder shows his VD in diamonds (by first bidding 3◇, then 3NT). Opener may now decide to bid 4♣, which is not forcing. Or, if more ambitious, opener bids 4◇, asking partner to choose his better major, despite the fact that opener knows the final contract will be a 4-3 fit. This 4◇ bid is called a 'choice of games cuebid' or, in this case, a 'choice of games VD cuebid'.

Suppose responder has a VD and a game force with a 4-card or 5-card major. You may want to add a VD option like this one to your structure:

Opener	Responder
1NT	2◇
2♡	3♣

Opener	Responder
1NT	2♣
2 any	3♣

In either sequence, 3♣ might be used to show 'game force + a VD'.

WHAT DO YOU LOSE BY PLAYING VACANT DOUBLETONS?

1) You lose something whenever you give up one meaning of an artificial bid for another.
2) You lose whenever fourth hand doubles and gets partner off to the killing lead.
3) You lose whenever you tell the defenders anything extra about your hands.
4) Finally, you may lose whenever you reach a contract other than 3NT that doesn't make, while if you had bid 1NT-3NT, the opening leader would not have found the lead of your VD suit.

Transfers at the Three-Level in Competition

One of the nice things about transfer responses to notrump bids is that you can 'right-side' the contract, protecting the strong hand's honors. When they compete over your notrump opening bid, must you be doomed to play from the wrong side? For example, playing IMPs, both vulnerable, you hold, as North:

♠ 9 8 3　♡ A K Q 10 4　◇ 8 6　♣ J 4 2

Partner	Oppt	You	Oppt
1NT	2♠	?	

In the semifinals of a knockout event, there were four different results on this deal.

At one table, North bid 3NT, reasoning that declaring the hand from his side would be hopeless (hence he did not want to show his hearts via Lebensohl). The whole deal was:

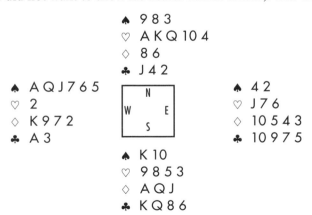

West led the ♠Q. Declarer pinned his hopes on the diamond finesse and went down three. At another table the bidding went:

West	North	East	South
			1NT
2♠	3♡	pass	4♡
dbl	all pass		

North-South were playing Lebensohl, the 'slow shows a stopper' version. This time West doubled! East led a spade and the defense played three rounds of spades. East was able to ruff in with his ♡J and return a diamond. Declarer finished down two, –500.

In the third match, North played 4♡ down two (undoubled). But at the fourth table, North-South scored up +620. How was this possible? This was their auction:

West	North	East	South
			1NT
2♠	3◊ [1]	pass	3♡
pass	3NT	pass	4♡
all pass			

1. 3◊ was a transfer to hearts.

West did his best by leading a trump. Declarer played three rounds of hearts and then took the diamond finesse. West won and returned a diamond. Declarer won and cashed a third diamond, pitching a spade from dummy. He next played a low club from hand. West was fixed. If he went up with the ace and got out with a club, declarer could pitch a second spade on the fourth round of clubs. If he ducked, declarer could win with the jack of clubs and play a second round of clubs to his king and West's ace. West was endplayed.

Here's how the transfers after competition work:

Opener	Oppt	Responder	Oppt
1NT	2 suit	?	
	dbl	I have a two notrump bid (8-9 points, no singletons)	
	2NT	transfer to clubs	
	3♣	transfer to diamonds	
	3◊	transfer to hearts	
	3♡	transfer to spades	
	3♠	minors, singleton in their suit	
	Cuebid	Stayman	

But wait — since all of the suits at the three-level are accounted for, which one is the cuebid? It's easiest to explain this with an example. Suppose they overcall 2♡:

Opener	Oppt	Responder	Oppt
1NT	2♡	3♡ [1]	
	1. Stayman.		

How, then, does responder transfer to spades? By bidding 3◊ — a transfer to their suit shows the next higher suit.

Let's try it again:

Opener	Oppt	Responder	Oppt
1NT	2◊[1]	?	

1. Natural.

Now:

3◊	=	Stayman
3♣	=	transfer to hearts

Opener	Oppt	Responder	Oppt
1NT	2♣[1]	?	

1. Natural.

Now:

3♣	=	Stayman
2NT	=	transfer to diamonds.

Other than the requirement to bid the suit requested, the transfer (to any suit) is not forcing and responder may be planning to pass at his next turn. Therefore, the opener must bid game if he thinks he can make it.

Opener	Oppt	Responder	Oppt
1NT	2◊[1]	2NT[2]	pass
?			

1. Natural.
2. Transfer to clubs.

With:

♠ A 4 2　♡ A 5 4　◊ A 4 3　♣ A 4 3 2

Opener bids 3NT (he's got nine tricks opposite king-sixth of clubs and out).

With:

♠ A 4 3　♡ A K 5 4　◊ A 4 3　♣ 4 3 2

he bids 3♣.

Opener	Oppt	Responder	Oppt
1NT	2◊[1]	3♣[2]	pass
?			

1. Natural.
2. Transfer to hearts..

With

♠ A 4 3　♡ A K 3 2　◊ A 3　♣ Q 10 6 5

he tries 4♡ — not sure it will make, but doesn't want to risk missing game opposite:

♠ J 2 ♡ Q J 7 6 5 ◇ 8 7 6 5 ♣ K 3

Suppose responder has a two-suiter. Using this convention, he can show both suits:

Opener	Oppt	Responder	Oppt
1NT	2◇[1]	3♣[2]	pass
3♡	pass	4♣[3]	pass
?			

1. Natural.
2. Transfer to hearts.
3. Natural.

Opener has:

♠ Q 9 4 2 ♡ A Q 5 ◇ A 2 ♣ K J 10 3

Opener can imagine slam if his partner has a singleton spade, so he cuebids 4◇. Partner cuebids 4♠, and opener jumps to 6♣. The entire deal:

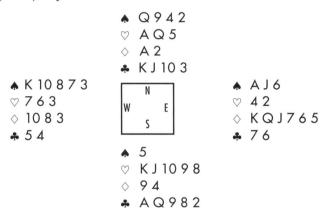

The entire auction was:

West	North	East	South
	1NT	2◇[1]	3♣[2]
pass	3♡	pass	4♣[3]
pass	4◇	pass	4♠
pass	6♣	all pass	

1. Natural.
2. Transfer to hearts.
3. Clubs.

Suppose you have 8-9 points, balanced. You double their overcall to show a 2NT bid. Partner can convert this to penalties with four trumps. This deal came up at matchpoints, with neither side vulnerable.

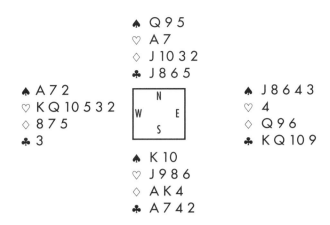

```
                      ♠ Q 9 5
                      ♡ A 7
                      ◇ J 10 3 2
                      ♣ J 8 6 5
  ♠ A 7 2                            ♠ J 8 6 4 3
  ♡ K Q 10 5 3 2      ┌─────────┐    ♡ 4
  ◇ 8 7 5             │    N    │    ◇ Q 9 6
  ♣ 3                 │ W     E │    ♣ K Q 10 9
                      │    S    │
                      └─────────┘
                      ♠ K 10
                      ♡ J 9 8 6
                      ◇ A K 4
                      ♣ A 7 4 2
```

West	North	East	South
			1NT
2♡	dbl[1]	pass[2]	pass
pass			

1. A natural 2NT bid.
2. Notice that East does not know if it's going to go 'all pass', or if South is going to bid something!

North leads the ◇J. If declarer ducks, North shifts to a spade. If declarer covers the diamond, three rounds of diamonds are played, followed by the spade shift. If declarer ducks the first spade, or wins the first spade and plays a club, North-South take two spades, two hearts, three diamonds and a club, for +500. If declarer wins the first spade and plays his king of hearts, North wins and plays a spade. Now South has to make a good play — ace and a club! Declarer can pitch away his spade loser, but will lose two more heart tricks; again +500.

Responding to Partner's 1NT Overcall – Dump 'System On'

For the last decade, tournament players have almost universally accepted the convention, **'System On'**, which means that when you make a direct one notrump overcall, your partner responds as if you had opened one notrump. This makes for a simple system to remember and that's about the only good reason for using this treatment.

The reason not to use 'System On' is that this usually includes transfers, and though you want to be declarer from the stronger side in principle, you have an even greater preference for the opponent with the stronger hand be on opening lead:

West	North	East	South
1♠	1NT	pass	?

```
                    ♠ K 3 2
                    ♡ A 9 4
                    ◇ A Q 8 4
                    ♣ A 3 2
    ♠ A Q 10 5 4    ┌───────┐      ♠ 9 7
    ♡ Q J 5         │   N   │      ♡ 7 6
    ◇ K 10 6        │ W   E │      ◇ 9 7 3 2
    ♣ Q 4           │   S   │      ♣ K 10 8 6 5
                    └───────┘
                    ♠ J 8 6
                    ♡ K 10 8 3 2
                    ◇ J 5
                    ♣ J 9 7
```

Notice that if South declares, West is on lead, and anything he does blows a trick. If South bids two diamonds, as a transfer to hearts, then North declares and East's spade lead sets up two quick spade tricks for the defense.

To get the opening bidder on lead, play:

West	North	East	South
1 suit	1NT	pass	?

2 of any	new suit to play
cuebid	Stayman
3 of a suit	natural and invitational

SUPER-SCIENCE VERSION

Use 2♣ for Stayman (you give up being able to play in two clubs, but that's all). The responses are:

2◇	four hearts (or 4-4 majors)
2♡	four spades
2♠	no major, minimum
2NT	no major, maximum

After his partner accepts the 'transfer' to a major, the notrump overcaller may pass or bid more with a maximum. Now you can stop at the two-level in a 4-4 fit on deals where the one-notrump bidder holds a minimum, and all suit contracts are played from the preferred side, putting the opening bidder on lead.

CUEBIDDING THEIR SUIT

The best use of the cuebid depends on which suit they opened:
* If they opened 1♣, 2♣ is still Stayman.
* If they opened 1◇, 2◇ can show short diamonds -- you are probably three-three in the majors, with a long club suit. Now you can find your way to a 5-3 major suit fit, a club contract, or a 4-3 major suit fit when partner's diamond stopper is weak.
* If they opened 1♡ or 1♠, you can use the cuebid to show shortness in their major, three of the other major, and 5-4 in the minors.

FINAL NOTE

You should still play 'front of card' when partner balances with one notrump. Now you want him to be declarer, as the opening bidder will be on lead.

The Trap Pass

The **Trap Pass** is not really a convention in the strictest sense, and it has therefore been over-looked in mainstream bridge literature.

The Trap Pass is sometimes a necessity, sometimes a choice. Say you hold a hand like:

♠ A 5 2 ♡ K Q 10 9 ◇ A 6 ♣ 9 8 7 3

If your RHO opens 1♡, you must pass, because double would be for takeout. Now suppose your LHO opened the bidding 1◇, partner passed, and righty bid 1♡. You could double for takeout, but the right action is to Trap Pass, hoping that the opponents get higher — in hearts, with luck.

West	North	East	South
1◇	pass	1♡	pass
1NT	pass	pass	dbl

This double says that South made a Trap Pass over 1♡ and would like to penalize 1NT. North should lead a heart. Remember, the double promises heart strength. This is the 'one-two punch' of the trap pass. First you pass and then you double 1NT.

If you sit South in the above auction, you cannot first pass 1♡ because you are too weak to compete, and then balance in the passout seat because now you don't want to sell out. Once you pass the first time, you must sell out if you don't hold the Trap Pass hand. Suppose you hold:

South (You)
- ♠ J 6 5 2
- ♡ 7 4
- ◇ A 5 3
- ♣ A 8 6 3

West	North	East	South
1◇	pass	1♡	pass
1NT	all pass!		

At your first chance to call, you hold the right shape to make a takeout double, but not enough strength. It won't be the end of the world if you quietly defend 1NT; sometimes that is your only chance to go plus. Sometimes East holds 9 or 10 points and if you balance, you go for a number. It is better to use this delayed double to obtain a 'number' yourself.

The Trap Pass allows you to collect the big score. In the Cavendish Invitational Pairs, against Brazilian star Gabriel Chagas, this auction occurred:

Both vul.

West	North	East	South
1♣	pass	1NT	pass
pass	dbl		

North held a strong hand with clubs:

♠ A 5 4   ♡ A Q J 10   ◇ 3 2   ♣ K Q J 9

Most of the other players in this position overcalled 1NT directly over 1♣ and ended in a partscore. South led a club because of the double, and North-South finished with +1100.

Here is another example from real life. In this case, West was Alvin Roth (see *Bridge Is a Partnership Game*, by Roth and Stone, hand #7 from the chapter called 'The Roth-Stone System in Action'). He held:

♠ A 10 6 3   ♡ K Q 7 6 4   ◇ Q 3   ♣ A Q

Alvin's RHO opened 1♡ and Alvin passed instead of making the busy bid of 1NT (letting them off the hook). Now the auction went:

(Roth)		*(Stone)*	
West	**North**	**East**	**South**
			1♡
pass	1NT	pass	pass
dbl	2♣	dbl	pass
pass	2♡	pass	pass
dbl	all pass		

This was the whole deal:

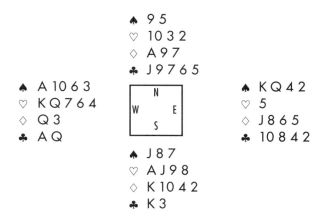

```
                      ♠ 9 5
                      ♡ 10 3 2
                      ◇ A 9 7
                      ♣ J 9 7 6 5
  ♠ A 10 6 3                              ♠ K Q 4 2
  ♡ K Q 7 6 4         ┌─────────┐         ♡ 5
  ◇ Q 3               │    N    │         ◇ J 8 6 5
  ♣ A Q              W│         │E        ♣ 10 8 4 2
                      │    S    │
                      └─────────┘
                      ♠ J 8 7
                      ♡ A J 9 8
                      ◇ K 10 4 2
                      ♣ K 3
```

Against 2♡ doubled, West led the ◇Q, and now declarer misguessed the hand and went for −1100 (playing perfectly, he can hold his loss to −500, which is still a poor result against East-West's partscore).

Of course, most players today would open 1◇ on the South cards, playing five-card majors. But if you exchange one of North's hearts with one of South's diamonds, the same scenario might still take place today.

Drop the Pre-Accept Bid

Opener	Responder
1NT	2NT
?	

For many years it has been popular to use 2NT as a transfer to 3◇ (and 2♠ as a transfer to 3♣). This enables the opener to pre-accept a game invitation based on his diamond holding, prime cards and stoppers for 3NT. Opener does this by bidding 3♣ over the transfer, instead of 3◇. (As an aside, there is a trend today to do the reverse, bid 3◇ with the hand that likes diamonds and 3♣ with the hand that has no interest. That way the strong hand gets to be declarer in the slam, if you get there.) Here's an extreme example of how well the method can work:

Opener	Responder
♠ 9 3 2	♠ 6
♡ A 5	♡ 7 6 2
◇ K 8 7 4	◇ A J 10 9 6 3 2
♣ A K Q J	♣ 4 3

Opener	Responder
1NT	2NT[1]
3♣[2]	3NT
4♣[3]	4♠[4]
4NT	5◇
6◇	pass

1. Transfer to diamonds.
2. Pre-accept — I like diamonds.
3. Cuebid (he can see 11 tricks now so slam is possible).
4. Happy to cooperate in view of the seventh diamond.

This pair reaches the laydown slam, while pairs playing in three notrump will probably go minus.

This is a more mundane example:

Opener	Responder
♠ A 5 4	♠ 7 3
♡ A 3	♡ 5 4 2
◇ K 7 6 2	◇ A J 9 8 5 3
♣ A 6 4 2	♣ 8 3

1NT	2NT[1]
3♣[2]	3NT[3]

1. Transfer to diamonds.
2. Pre-accept.
3. Responder takes a shot at three notrump and the 20-point game rolls home.

WHAT DO YOU LOSE PLAYING PRE-ACCEPTS?

This is great when it works, but how often do these situations occur? What do you give up in order to cater to this situation? In what way does this convention backfire? There are a number of issues.

1. You have to give up the direct raise to 2NT with 8-9 points, invitational hand.
2. Therefore, to show the invite you must bid Stayman whether or not you have a four-card major (followed by 2NT). This reveals gratuitous information about declarer's hand, allowing the opponents to defend more accurately. It also potentially allows the opponents to get into the auction where before they couldn't — they can double Stayman, for example, or slip in a bid at the two-level, which they can't do after 1NT – 2NT.
3. Even the pre-accept bid itself can let them in! Here's an example from Andrew Robson:

Both vul.

```
                          ♠ 9 8 6
                          ♡ 6 2
                          ◇ A 8 6 5 4 2
                          ♣ 9 3
```

Zia   **Andrew**
```
♠ 4 3                                                ♠ Q 7 5 2
♡ K 9 8             N                                ♡ A Q J 7 5
◇ 10 9          W       E                            ◇ 3
♣ A 10 8 7 6 5      S                                ♣ K J 2
```
```
                          ♠ A K J 10
                          ♡ 10 4 3
                          ◇ K Q J 7
                          ♣ Q 4
```

This is one of the two final boards that helped Andrew (who was playing with Zia Mahmood) win the 2000 Cap Gemini tournament. Aided by the dreaded pre-accept by an opponent, Andrew and Zia were the only pair in the strong field to reach the vulnerable four-heart game East-West!

West	North	East	South
			1NT
pass	2NT[1]	pass	3♣[2]
dbl	3◇	dbl[3]	pass
3♡	pass	4♡	all pass

1. Transfer to diamonds.
2. Pre-accept (a questionable decision).
3. Takeout (i.e., majors).

Many East-West pairs reached five clubs down one, and one pair reached four clubs, making (to win five IMPs). But the good four-heart game was difficult to reach unless West could get into the bidding via a double of that 3♣ bid. Suppose the bidding goes:

West	North	East	South
			1NT
pass	3♣[1]	pass	3◇
pass	pass	dbl	pass
?			

1. Transfer to diamonds.

It's true that West could bid three hearts, but will he? He is much more likely to bid his six-card suit than his three-card suit!

Give up the pre-accept bid in diamonds. One notrump-two notrump should be natural, with three clubs the transfer to three diamonds. You might lose out once in a while, but not necessarily. For example, on the first example hand:

Opener	Responder
♠ 9 3 2	♠ 6
♡ A 5	♡ 7 6 2
◇ K 8 7 4	◇ A J 10 9 6 3 2
♣ A K Q J	♣ 4 3

After opener's 1NT bid, responder transfers to diamonds (via 3♣) and opener bids 3♡. This should show a massive hand for diamonds, a heart card, and express doubt about the other major (spades). Now if responder bids 4♠ (splinter) on the way to 5◇, that's all opener needs to hear.

Second example:

Opener	Responder
♠ A 5 4	♠ 7 3
♡ A 3	♡ 5 4 2
◇ K 7 6 2	◇ A J 9 8 5 3
♣ A 6 4 2	♣ 8 3

1NT	3♣[1]
3NT[2]	

1. Transfer to diamonds.
2. !

Why not? Opener is allowed to evaluate his cards. He sees he has all the suits stopped plus a tremendous diamond fit. He merely needs ace-sixth of diamonds from partner. If responder has something like jack-seventh of diamonds and out, he pulls to four diamonds. The worst that can happen is three diamonds makes exactly nine tricks, four diamonds fails by a trick, and you lose a partscore swing.

Wasting the natural two notrump bid to cater to an infrequent situation, which can be dealt with via natural bidding anyway, makes no sense.

Roth 4♣ Response to Preempts

This convention caters to our modern light preempts, where responder, holding a huge hand and interest in slam, wants to find out how light partner really is before getting too high.

Opener	Responder
3 suit	4♣

In response to an opening three-level bid, 4♣ is a slam try and asks opener to tell about his preempt via artificial steps:

4♦	**a bad suit and bad hand**
4♡	**2 of the top 3 honors in the preempt suit**
4♠	**good hand but broken suit**
4NT	**solid suit**

This marvelous convention was invented by Alvin Roth. It is incredibly useful, because it frees up all the other bids and they can be natural and not forcing. So now 3♠-4♡ is natural and to play, and 3♦-3♡ and 3♦-3♠ are natural and forward-going but not forcing. Here's another nice benefit:

Opener	Responder
3♠	4♣[1]
4♦[2]	4♡

1. Roth.
2. Bad hand, bad suit.

The 4♡ bid here can be used as natural and not forcing. Suppose responder holds:

♠ Q 4 ♡ A K Q J 6 4 ◇ A Q 10 3 ♣ 6

Partner opens 3♠ and there are slam possibilities, since partner is allowed to have the ace-king of spades. But once opener shows a bad suit and bad hand, it might be better to play in 4♡. You can bid it and partner can pass or correct. Partner will pass 4♡ with something like:

♠ A 8 7 6 5 3 2 ♡ 7 5 ◇ J 4 ♣ 5 2

Here 4♡ is cold whereas 4♠ can go down on a bad day (if the diamond king is offside, the opponents could take a diamond, a club, and two spades).

The 4♣ bid can also be used to set up Keycard Blackwood. Since we play Keycard Blackwood only when a suit has been bid and raised (see page 106), 3♠-4NT is not Keycard Blackwood. To set up Keycard, you bid 4♣ over 3♠; if you next bid 4NT, it's now Keycard Blackwood.

There's another slight wrinkle you can add when the opening preempt is in clubs. Instead of wasting a whole level of the auction with 4♣ immediately, play that 3◇ over 3♣ is forcing, asking for length in a major. If you bid 3◇ and follow-up with 4♣, it's forcing and a slam try (just like the 4♣ bid over 3◇, 3♡ or 3♠). This frees up the 4♣ direct raise over 3♣ as a natural call.

Here's an example:

Opener	Responder
♠ 10 8 6 5	♠ A K J 3
♡ 3	♡ A K 8 4
◇ 9 8	◇ 4 2
♣ K Q 9 6 5 3	♣ A 4 2
3♣	3◇
3♠	4♠
pass	

Notice that while 3NT will fail after a diamond lead and 5♣ will fail if the queen of spades is offside, 4♠ is a great spot.

Double Keycard Blackwood

Double Keycard Blackwood* is extremely valuable for slam bidding and especially important in locating grand slams. It comes up whenever two suits have been bid and raised. For example:

Partner	You
1♠	2♣
3♣	3♠

The two hands are:

♠ A Q 6 5 3	♠ K J 7
♡ 9 2	♡ A 4
◇ J 3	◇ A 5
♣ K Q J 6	♣ A 9 8 7 4 3

As you can see, 7NT is cold, barring a 5-0 spade break. When partner raises your clubs, you can see that a grand slam is possible if partner has the missing honors in the black suits (you will pitch your losing red cards on partner's fourth and fifth spades). How can you investigate? Set up Double Keycard Blackwood first, by raising partner's suit. The bidding continues:

Partner	You
1♠	2♣
3♣	3♠
4♠	4NT
?	

---

* There is much in common between this convention and the vastly more complex and well-named Byzantine Blackwood, described by its inventor Jack Marx in *Bridge Magazine* in 1972.

The responses to Double Keycard Blackwood are:

5♣	**0 or 3 keycards (of six: the four aces, and the kings in your two suits)**
5♦	**1 or 4 keycards**
5♡	**2 keycards; neither trump queen**
5♠	**2 keycards plus the trump queen in the lower-ranking agreed suit**
5NT	**2 keycards plus the trump queen in the higher-ranking agreed suit**
6♣	**2 keycards; plus both trump queens.**

Thus, our auction in full is:

Partner	You
1♠	2♣
3♣	3♠
4♠	4NT
6♣	7NT

You might even want to set up Double Keycard Blackwood by raising partner's suit with a doubleton! Suppose partner opens with one heart and you hold:

♠ A K Q 6 5 2   ♡ A 4   ♦ K Q 2   ♣ J 3

Do not make a strong jump shift (even if you play them)! You will use up too much room and you won't be able to use Double Keycard Blackwood. Start slowly with a 1♠ response. The auction continues:

Partner	You
1♡	1♠
2♠	3♡¹
4♡	4NT²
5♣³	7♠

1. Forcing.
2. Double KB.
3. 0 or 3 keycards.

Partner's hand is:

♠ J 10 4   ♡ K J 7 6 5   ♦ A 4   ♣ A 6 3

THE QUEEN-ASK AFTER DOUBLE KEYCARD BLACKWOOD

After a 5♣ or 5♦ response, the next higher bid that is not one of your suits asks about queens. The responses are:

step 1	**no queen**
step 2	**lower queen**
step 3	**higher queen**
anything else	**both queens**

On our example hand,

♠ A K Q 6 5 2 ♡ A 4 ◇ K Q 2 ♣ J 3

Partner	You
1♡	1♠
2♠	3♡
4♡	4NT
5♣	?

you can ask for queens with 5◇. If partner's hand is

♠ J 10 4 ♡ K Q 7 6 5 ◇ A 4 ♣ A 6 3

he now bids 5♠, showing the queen of hearts (the lower-ranking key queen — 5♡ would show no queens, 5NT the spade queen). Now you can bid seven notrump rather than seven spades.

ALERT!

Double Key Card Blackwood is only used when two suits have been explicitly bid and raised. No inferences count! The suits must be bid and raised:

Partner	You
1♠	2♡
3♡	3♠
4♠	4NT[1]

1. Double KB.

Partner	You
1♠	2◇
2♡	3♠
4♡	4NT[1]

1. KB for spades only.

Partner	You
1♠	2◇
3◇	3♡
4♠	4NT[1]

1. KB for diamonds only.

Partner	You
♠ K 4 2	♠ A Q J 9 8
♡ 9 3	♡ A 8
◇ A 10 8	◇ 5
♣ K Q 9 8 2	♣ A J 10 7 3

1♣	1♠
2♠	3♣
3◇	4NT[1]
5♣[2]	5◇[3]
5♠[4]	7♣

1. Double KB: spades and clubs were bid and raised.
2. 0 or 3.
3. Queen ask.
4. Lower queen.

Partner	You
♠ A Q 9 2	♠ 6
♡ Q 5 4	♡ A K J 2
◇ K J 5 2	◇ A 8 7 6 4 3
♣ 8 4	♣ A 9

1◇	1♡
1♠	3◇[1]
3♡	4♣
4♡	4NT[2]
5NT[3]	7◇

1. Forcing.
2. Double KB for diamonds and hearts.
3. Two keycards plus the queen of hearts (higher ranking queen).

You have deduced that partner has four diamonds because he showed 4-3 in the majors; with 4-3-3-3 he opens one club. Therefore he is 4-3-4-2 or 4-3-5-1 and seven diamonds is an excellent spot. It's very handy to be able to find out exactly which queen he has!

Bridge Conventions in Depth

Exclusion Blackwood

This exotic tool is used mainly by Keycard Blackwood fans, but can be used with plain Blackwood as well. The idea is that you want to ask for aces but you hold a void, and so you need to know how many aces partner holds outside of your void suit.

Exclusion Blackwood works like this:

After a suit is bid and raised, you make a double jump in a new suit. Double jumps begin with the 11th bid from the previous bid.

Example:

Partner	You
1♦	1♡
2♡	?

Count the steps, and you'll find that 4♡ is the tenth bid above 2♡. So:

4♠   **Exclusion Blackwood with a void in spades**

5♣   **Exclusion Blackwood with a void in clubs**

Also, some play:

5♦   **Exclusion Blackwood with a void in diamonds**

This last idea is a little dangerous because partner opened the bidding in diamonds. Eddie Kantar, author of a book on Keycard Blackwood, said, 'I have always been leery about using Exclusion in a suit partner has bid. In my book it can't be done and in real life I have never done it although I have wanted to several times. Too scary. However, if you wish to promote that idea, the rules have to be crystal clear.'

Suppose you hold:

♠ A   ♡ K 10 9 8 6 5 4   ◇ K Q J 5 2   ♣ —

Partner	You
1◇	1♡
2♡	?

You bid 5♣, showing a void in clubs and asking for aces. Partner will not count the ace of clubs in his reply. He will bid 5◇ with no aces, 5♡ with one working ace (heart ace or diamond ace), and 5♠ with two working aces.

Keycard Blackwood players will use the same tool but count 'keycards' instead of just plain aces. Try this hand:

♠ A K 4   ♡ A 8 7 5 2   ◇ K Q 7 6 5   ♣ —

Partner	You
1◇	1♡
2♡	5♣
5◇ [1]	pass

1. No working keycards (your side is missing the ace of diamonds and the king of hearts).

Partner	You
1◇	1♡
2♡	5♣
5♡ [1]	6◇

1. One working keycard (king of hearts or ace of diamonds).

Partner	You
1◇	1♡
2♡	5♣
5♠ [1]	6◇

1. Two working keycards without the queen of hearts.

Partner	You
1♦	1♡
2♡	5♣
5NT[1]	7♦

1. Two working keycards with the queen of hearts.

Question: Can you use Exclusion Blackwood with a simple jump?

Answer: Yes, if the jump is to the five-level.

Opener	Responder
1♡	1♠
2♦	3♡
5♣	

Opener has:

♠ K 4 ♡ K Q 7 6 5 4 ◇ K Q J 3 2 ♣ —

Question: Can you make an Exclusion Blackwood bid without an agreed trump suit?

Answer: Yes, if the jump is 11+ bids, and you and partner have made at least three bids prior to the jump.

♠ — ♡ A K Q 5 2 ◇ K J 6 5 ♣ K 8 4 3

Opener	Responder
1♣	1♡
2♣	4♠

Is 4♠ Exclusion Blackwood? The answer, according to our formula, is yes.

Warning: You pick up

♠ K Q J 7 6 3 ♡ Q J 10 5 4 2 ◇ 8 ♣ —

Opener	Responder
1♣	1♠
2♣	?

Don't bid 4♡! According to the formula, that's Exclusion Blackwood. So if you play this convention, you'll have to bid 2♡ or 3♡, whichever is natural and forcing in your system.

TEXAS AND EXCLUSION

Another application for Exclusion Blackwood occurs after Texas Transfers. Many partnerships use a new suit after Texas as Exclusion Blackwood.

Opener	Responder
1NT	4♢ [1]
4♡	4♠ [2]

1. Transfer to hearts.
2. Exclusion Blackwood, void in spades.

WHAT DO YOU LOSE BY PLAYING THIS CONVENTION?

Nothing, in theory. But you must remember when a jump is natural and when it's Exclusion.

Specific King-Ask

In standard bidding, after asking for aces with Blackwood, 5NT asks for kings:

Opener	Responder
1♡	3♡
4NT	5♡ [1]
5NT	?

1. Two aces.

Opener finds out that responder holds two aces, and he next bids 5NT, guaranteeing all the aces and asking for kings. The 5NT Specific King-Ask asks responder which king or kings he holds, rather than the number of kings.

Suppose the trump suit is spades:

Opener	Responder
1♠	3♠
4NT	5♡ [1]
5NT	?

1. Two aces.

Now:

6♣	**king of clubs**
6♢	**king of diamonds**
6♡	**king of hearts**
6♠	**no side-suit kings**
6NT	**all the side-suit kings**

Example #1:

Opener	Responder
♠ K Q 7 6 3 2	♠ A 9 8 4
♡ A Q 5	♡ K 7 6 3
◇ 7	◇ A 4 3 2
♣ A 4 2	♣ 6

Using regular Blackwood, the auction goes:

1♠	4♣[1]
4NT	5♡[2]
5NT	6◇[3]
?	

1. Splinter.
2. Two aces.
3. One king.

Opener doesn't know which king responder has.

Using Specific King-Ask 5NT:

Opener	Responder
1♠	4♣[1]
4NT	5♡[2]
5NT	6♡[3]
7♠	

1. Splinter.
2. Two aces.
3. King of hearts.

Example #2

Opener	Responder
♠ 4	♠ A 6 5
♡ A K J 8 7 3	♡ Q 10 9 6 2
◇ A Q 6 5 4	◇ K 7 2
♣ A	♣ 9 3
1♡	3♡
4NT	5◇
5NT	6◇ [1]
7♡	pass

1. King of diamonds.

The King-Ask is not recommended for minor-suit slams because the specific king may be higher than the trump suit:

Opener	Responder
♠ A	♠ K 5 4
♡ 6	♡ A 8
◇ A K J 8 7 3	◇ Q 10 9 6 4
♣ A Q 6 5 2	♣ 8 7 4
1◇	2◇
4NT	5◇
5NT	6♠
oops	

If hearts is the trump suit, the King-Ask will work as long as the king you are looking for is not the king of spades. When playing the King-Ask for hearts, it's a good idea to agree not to show the king of spades. That way, if opener is looking for a specific king, at least he can use the King-Ask successfully two out of three times (i.e., he can find out about the club king or diamond king, but not the spade king). So:

Opener	Responder
1♡	4♡
4NT	5◇
5NT	6♡ [1]

1. No minor suit king, but doesn't deny the king of spades.

SUPER-SCIENCE VARIATION

For those who want it all, you can ask for a specific king below the 5NT level when spades are not trumps.

If you play regular Blackwood, the suit above the trump suit is the King-Ask. For spades, you already have enough room (as demonstrated above). For the other suits, it works this way:

Opener	Responder
1♡	4♡
4NT	5♢
5♡[1]	

1. Sign-off.

Opener	Responder
1♡	4♡
4NT	5♢
5♠[1]	

1. King-Ask.

Now:

5NT   **king of spades (unbiddable king)**

6♣   **king of clubs**

6♢   **king of diamonds**

6♡   **no king**

Opener	Responder
1♢	3♢
4NT	5♢
5♡[1]	

1. King-Ask.

Now:

5♠   **king of spades**

5NT   **king of hearts (unbiddable king)**

6♣   **king of clubs**

6♢   **no king**

Bridge Conventions in Depth

More difficult is this sequence:

Opener	Responder
1♣	3♣
4NT	5◊
5♡[1]	

1. King-Ask.

Now:

5♠   **king of spades**

5NT   **king of diamonds or king of hearts (two unbiddable kings!)**

6♣   **no king**

The only way around this one is to use the Redwood convention instead of 4NT Blackwood. Then, when clubs are agreed, 4◊ asks for aces, not 4NT:

Opener	Responder
1♣	3♣
4◊[1]	4NT[2]
5◊[3]	

1. Redwood.
2. Two aces.
3. King-Ask.

Now:

5♡   **king of hearts**

5♠   **king of spades**

5NT   **king of diamonds (unbiddable king)**

6♣   **no king**

THE KING-ASK WITH KEYCARD BLACKWOOD

If you play Keycard Blackwood, the 'Queen-Ask' sometimes takes up the next step, so you may not be able to find out about the 'unbiddable' specific king:

Opener	Responder
1♡	4♡
4NT	5♢

If this is a Keycard sequence, then 5♡ would be a sign-off, while 5♠ would normally be the Queen-Ask. If you have the queen of trumps, you bid a specific king over the Queen-Ask:

Opener	Responder
1♡	4♡
4NT	5♢
5♠	

5NT — **queen of trumps plus no king or an unbiddable king (spades); 6♣ now asks which and 6♡ says no king.**

6♣ — **queen of trumps plus king of clubs**

6♢ — **queen of trumps plus king of diamonds**

6♡ — **no queen of trumps**

If opener has the queen of trumps and simply wants to locate a specific king, he must bid 5NT over 5♢:

Opener	Responder
1♡	4♡
4NT	5♢
5NT[1]	

1. King-Ask.

Once again, you cannot find out about the king of spades. This is why some use 4♠ as Keycard Blackwood when hearts is the trump suit.

There is also an issue when diamonds are agreed, although you can still distinquish the Queen-Ask from the King-Ask:

Opener	Responder
1♢	3♢
4NT	5♢
?	

5♡ — **asks about the queen of trumps**

5♠ — **King-Ask**

Opener	Responder
1♦	3♦
4NT	5♦
5♠	

5NT   **king of hearts or king of spades**

6♣   **king of clubs**

6♦   **no king**

Again, you cannot know for sure over 5NT which it is (unless you have the other one).

When clubs is the trump suit, and you use 'traditional' Keycard Blackwood, you can't find out about specific kings:

Opener	Responder
1♣	3♣
4NT	5♦
?	

5♡   **Queen-Ask**

5♠   **King-Ask**

Opener	Responder
1♣	3♣
4NT	5♦
5♠	?

5NT   **one king**

6♣   **no kings**

Again, Redwood helps:

Opener	Responder
1♣	3♣
4♦	?

4NT   **two key cards without the queen**

5♣   **sign-off**

5♦   **King-Ask (because trump queen is known)**

Opener	Responder
1♣	3♣
4♦	4NT
5♦	?

5♡   **king of hearts**

5♠   **king of spades**

5NT   **king of diamonds**

There are ways around the problem of two unbiddable kings, but that would involve adding a second type of king-ask over the first reply (for example, when 5♠ is the king-ask, 5NT is also a king-ask but only for the highest ranking 'unbiddable king'). Complicating your system, however, is perhaps not worth the rare advantage of this second king-ask idea. Anyway, here it is:

Opener	Responder
1♦	3♦
4NT	5♦
?	

5♡   **Queen-Ask**

5♠   **King-Ask for the king of hearts (5NT) or king of clubs (6♣)**

5NT   **King-Ask only for the king of spades**

You see how complicated it can get!

Finally, what do you do when you need two kings for a grand slam? The answer is to use the King-Ask and then bid again under the trump suit.

Opener	Responder
1♡	3♡
4NT	5♠
5NT	6♣
6♦ [1]	

1. Need another one, partner!

And if you need two specific kings (and not the third king), well, maybe you shouldn't have bid Blackwood to begin with!

52

The Squeeze Bid (aka 'Last Train to Clarkesville')

Ever have a hand where you don't feel safe going past game, but you hate to sign off? Try the Squeeze Bid (some call this convention *Last Train* or *Last Train to Clarkesville*).

Here's a hand from real life where North-South missed a great slam:

Neither vul.

```
          ♠ 7 2
          ♡ Q 7 4 3 2
          ◇ A Q 6 4 3 2
          ♣ —
              N
          W       E
              S
          ♠ A K 4
          ♡ K 10 9 8 6
          ◇ J
          ♣ J 10 5 2
```

West	North	East	South
		1♣	1♡
pass	4♣	pass	?

South doesn't exactly have the world's fair, but he does have both unbid suits controlled, nothing wasted in clubs, and decent trumps. What should he do? In real life, he signed off. North couldn't go anywhere because there was no safety at the five level (switch South's spades and clubs, for example).

SOLUTION

The easy and safe solution is for South to bid four diamonds — a Squeeze Bid. This is an artificial bid that says nothing about diamonds. It simply means, 'Partner, I have too much to sign off and not enough to bid past game.'

North tries again with 5♣ and now, knowing North has a club void, South happily bids slam.

Here's another example:

Opener	Responder
1♠	3♠[1]
4◇	4♡[2]

1. Limit.
2. Not a cuebid; this is a squeeze bid.

The hands were:

♠ A K 9 8 2	♠ Q J 7 3
♡ 9	♡ J 6 4 2
◇ A Q J 10 3	◇ K 7
♣ Q 8	♣ A 10 3

Responder does not want to sign off with a four-spade bid. After all, his spades and hearts could be reversed. In addition, he has the big king of diamonds for his partner and the ace of clubs. On the other hand, he hasn't enough to go past game by himself, so he makes a squeeze bid.

If opener is playing a style of cuebids where he denied a club honor when he bid 4◇, responder must have one (otherwise he knows his side is off the ace-king of clubs and he'll sign off in 4♠ rather than make a squeeze bid). If opener has not denied a club honor, opener reasons as follows, 'My partner has either the ace of hearts or ace of clubs — he would hardly make a squeeze bid missing all five keycards! I will bid 5♡ now, which surely is an indication that I have no club control. If my partner's ace is in hearts, he will sign off in five spades; if his ace is in clubs, he will bid slam for us.'

Bridge Conventions in Depth

ALERT!

Be careful — you cannot make a squeeze bid in their suit. For example:

Partner	Oppt	You	Oppt
1♠	2◇	2♡	pass
2♠	pass	3♣	pass
4♣	pass	?	

You hold:

♠ 4   ♡ A K J 7 5   ◇ 8 2   ♣ A K 8 6 3

Neither 4♡ and 4♠ is forcing; so you'd rather do something else — but you cannot bid 4◇, squeeze bid. Since diamonds is the opponents' suit, 4◇ here is a cuebid. What is the solution? You can bid 4♡ and hope partner bids again with the appropriate hand; if he bids 4♠ over 4♡, you bid 5♣ and this should indicate that you are looking for a diamond control. Or you can bid 5♣ and hope partner will bid six with queen-fourth of clubs and two aces.

4♠ Means 'Please Blackwood'

53

PREVIEW

Playing IMPs, both sides vulnerable, you hold:

♠ Q 2   ♡ A J 7 5 2   ◊ A K 9 2   ♣ 8 3

Partner	You
1♣	1♡
2◊	3◊
4♡	?

You have no idea how many tricks your side can take on this hand. Your partner seems to be showing a great three-card heart raise plus a maximum reverse. What should you do? It won't help you to Blackwood, because you have no idea where to go. You don't even have a spade control and suppose he has

♠ 10 4   ♡ K Q 6   ◊ Q J 7   ♣ A K Q J 10

What you would really like to do is to tell your partner about your three big keycards and let him decide.

THE SOLUTION

The solution is to bid 4♠, which means, '**Partner, Please Blackwood.**' This is not a cuebid because with first- or second-round control of spades you would bid Blackwood yourself. So 4♠ therefore means, 'I'm not sure what to do. I have a very big hand for this auction and I think it's safe to go past game.' The bidding continues:

Fine Arts Conventions

Partner	You
1♣	1♡
2◇	3◇
4♡	4♠[1]
4NT[2]	5♣[3]
7◇	

1. Please Blackwood.
2. Double Keycard Blackwood for diamonds and hearts.
3. Three keycards.

Here are both hands:

Partner	You
♠ A	♠ Q 2
♡ K Q 8	♡ A J 7 5 2
◇ Q J 10 3	◇ A K 9 2
♣ A K 10 5 4	♣ 8 3

Partner now knows you have five hearts and four diamonds (with 4-4 and a good hand, you would have responded 1◇ and not 1♡). You have the ♡A and ◇A-K. You do not have three clubs and one spade because you would have bid 3♣ over his reverse or used Blackwood over 4♡. Therefore you have two or three spades and he can just about take 7◇ to the bank because a spade ruff in his hand will provide the thirteenth trick.

(By the way, if partner had the aforementioned

♠ 10 4   ♡ K Q 6   ◇ Q J 7   ♣ A K Q J 10

he would not bid Blackwood; he would bid 5♣. He would reason that if his partner holds the ace of hearts, the ace-king of diamonds and a spade control, he'll bid a slam himself. So it's possible that after we bid Please Blackwood, partner might respond with a non-Blackwood bid, which means, 'I also don't have a suitable hand for Blackwood, so instead I'll describe my hand to you a little more, and you can decide what to do.')

Four spades is specifically the Please Blackwood bid because lower-ranking suits are used for the squeeze bid (see page 217). More examples of Please Blackwood follow.

You hold:

♠ A 4 2   ♡ A K 6 3   ◇ A 7 2   ♣ A 5 4

Partner	You
1♡	3♡[1]
4◇	4♠[2]

1. Forcing (or insert your favorite forcing raise here).
2. Please Blackwood.

This is an extreme example, but the point is that if partner knows you have all of the key cards, he may be able to bid a grand slam with something like:

♠ K 6 ♡ Q J 7 5 2 ◇ K Q J 5 4 ♣ 9

You certainly can't count thirteen tricks, but partner can.
Another example:

Partner	You
♠ A 6 3	♠ 7 2
♡ Q J	♡ A K 8 7 5 2
◇ A 9	◇ 8 3 2
♣ K Q J 10 7 4	♣ A 6

Partner	You
1♣	1♡
3♣	3♡
4♡	4♠
4NT[1]	5♣[2]
7NT	

1. Keycard Blackwood for hearts (the only suit that was bid and raised).
2. 0 or 3 keycards.

Again, you can't count tricks, but partner can.
Be careful, though — if four spades could be natural, it is!

Partner	You
1♡	1♠
4♡	4♠

It might be tempting to play this as Please Blackwood but you could have been dealt:

Partner	You
♠ —	♠ A Q J 10 9 8 7 6
♡ A K Q 8 6 4 2	♡ —
◇ A 6 4	◇ 8 7 3
♣ K 5 2	♣ Q 6

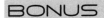
BONUS

How do you bid Please Blackwood if the trump suit is spades? You can't, so you 'zoom' — that is, you show your partner how many aces you have without anyone having bid Blackwood!

Partner	You
♠ Q 8 7 5 4 2	♠ A K 10 3
♡ A 5	♡ 9 7 6
◇ Q 3	◇ A K 4
♣ A K 5	♣ 6 4 2

1♠	3♠[1]
4♣	4◇
4♡	?

1. Forcing.

You'd certainly like to do more than bid 4♠ because your partner cuebid twice missing the ace-king of trump. However, you have no idea if a slam is on. The solution is to 'zoom' - that is, show partner how many keycards you hold and let him decide. The auction continues:

Partner	You
1♠	3♠[1]
4♣	4◇
4♡	5♣[2]
5NT	6◇[3]
6♠	pass

1. Forcing.
2. Zero or three keycards.
3. One king.

Bidding after 1◇–1M; 3◇–?

54

PREVIEW

One of the most difficult constructive auctions occurs when you open the bidding 1◇ and rebid 3◇ over partner's 1♡ or 1♠ response. At this point, responder may want to:

1) *rebid his suit;*

2) *show a club stopper; or*

3) *show a stopper in the other major.*

But there are only two bids available under 3NT. Two bids — three meanings. What to do?

THE SOLUTION

The following solution is a variation of a method invented by Benito Garozzo.

Opener	Responder
1◇	1♡ / 1♠
3◇	?

3♡   **a rebid of the first-bid major or a stopper in the unbid major**
3♠   **a stopper in clubs**

Over 3♡, opener may bid 3♠ to ask. Now 3NT shows the major stopper, while a four-level bid shows that responder was rebidding his suit.

Opener	Responder
1♢	1♡
3♢	3♡[1]
3♠[2]	3NT[3]

1. Rebiddable hearts, or a spade stopper.
2. Which?
3. Spade stopper.

Opener	Responder
1♢	1♡
3♢	3♡[1]
3♠[2]	4♣[3]

1. Rebiddable hearts, or a spade stopper.
2. Which?
3. Rebiddable hearts, plus something in clubs.

Opener	Responder
1♢	1♡
3♢	3♡[1]
3♠[2]	4♢[3]

1. Rebiddable hearts, or a spade stopper.
2. Which?
3. Rebiddable hearts, plus diamond support.

Opener	Responder
1♢	1♡
3♢	3♡[1]
3♠[2]	4♡[3]

1. Rebiddable hearts, or a spade stopper.
2. Which?
3. Rebiddable hearts, nothing else to say.

Opener	Responder
1♢	1♠
3♢	3♡[1]
3♠[2]	4♣[3]

1. Rebiddable spades, or a heart stopper.
2. Which?
3. Rebiddable spades, plus something in clubs.

Opener	Responder
1◇	1♠
3◇	3♡[1]
3♠[2]	4◇[3]

1. Rebiddable spades, or a heart stopper.
2. Which?
3. Rebiddable spades, plus diamond support.

Opener	Responder
1◇	1♠
3◇	3♡[1]
3♠[2]	4♡[3]

1. Rebiddable spades, or a heart stopper.
2. Which?
3. Rebiddable spades, plus something in hearts.

Opener	Responder
1◇	1♠
3◇	3♡[1]
3♠[2]	4♠[3]

1. Rebiddable spades, or a heart stopper.
2. Which?
3. Rebiddable spades, nothing else to say.

Bridge Conventions in Depth

Example #1

Opener	Responder
♠ A 5	♠ K 8 7 3
♡ 9 2	♡ A 6 5
◇ A K J 10 8 3	◇ Q 4
♣ K Q 6	♣ 7 5 3 2

1◇	1♠
3◇	3♡[1]
3♠[2]	3NT[3]
pass	

1. Rebiddable spades, or a heart stopper.
2. Which?
3. Heart stopper.

Example #2

Opener	Responder
♠ A 4	♠ K Q 7 6 5 3
♡ 9 2	♡ Q 7
◇ A K J 10 4 2	◇ Q 6
♣ K Q 6	♣ 7 5 3

1◇	1♠
3◇	3♡[1]
3♠[2]	4♠[3]
pass	

1. Rebiddable spades, or a heart stopper.
2. Which?
3. Rebiddable spades, nothing further.

Example #3

Suppose responder had bid 3♠ showing a club stopper. Opener would have to retreat to the four-level. Now the bid of 4♣ with the strong fragment would be best:

Opener	Responder
♠ A 4	♠ K 6 5 3
♡ 9 2	♡ 7 4
◇ A K J 10 4 2	◇ 6 3
♣ K Q 6	♣ A J 7 5 3

Opener	Responder
1◇	1♠
3◇	3♠¹
4♣	5♣
pass	

1. Club stopper.

WHAT IF THEY INTERFERE?

If the artificial 3♡ or 3♠ bid is doubled, you should thank your opponent. You now have more room to maneuver.

First, redouble is natural with strength in that suit.

Opener	Responder
♠ A 5 2	♠ Q 6
♡ K 4	♡ Q 10 8 3
◇ A K Q 7 6 3	◇ 8 5 4
♣ Q 7	♣ A 10 3 2

Opener	Oppt	Responder	Oppt
1◇	pass	1♡	pass
3◇	pass	3♠¹	dbl
redbl²	pass	3NT	

1. Club stopper.
2. Spade stopper.

Clearly, you want to play 3NT from the responder's side.

If responder has denied a stopper in the other major, he can now redouble with a partial stopper:

Opener		Responder	
♠ J 5 2		♠ Q 6	
♡ A 4		♡ Q 10 8 3	
◇ A K Q 7 6 3		◇ 8 5 4	
♣ K 7		♣ A 10 3 2	

Opener	Oppt	Responder	Oppt
1◇	pass	1♡	pass
3◇	pass	3♠[1]	dbl
pass	pass	redbl[2]	pass
3NT			

1. Club stopper.
2. Partial spade stopper.

Here's a final, fairly sophisticated, example:

Opener		Responder	
♠ A 5		♠ K Q 7 2	
♡ 7 6 5		♡ A 8 3	
◇ A K Q 8 6 2		◇ 5 4 3	
♣ K 9		♣ 7 4 2	

Opener	Oppt	Responder	Oppt
1◇	pass	1♡	pass
3◇	pass	3♡[1]	dbl
pass	pass	redbl[2]	pass
3NT[3]			

1. Rebiddable spade suit or heart stopper.
2. Full stopper (he has not denied a stopper earlier, as per the previous example), 'but no need to play the notrump from my side.'
3. 'Better play the notrump from my side then, to protect my king of clubs.'

New Suit 2NT

You pick up:

♠ A 9 8 7   ♡ Q 8 7 5   ◊ K 2   ♣ A J 2

Partner opens 1♣. You respond 1♡. Partner rebids 2♣.

Partner	You
1♣	1♡
2♣	?

What is your next call?

THE SOLUTION

New Suit 2NT means that when responder bids 2NT at his second turn (after first responding in a new suit), it's like bidding another new suit — it's natural and forcing, showing 10 or more points. This applies after opener has rebid anything but 1NT.

The following formula demonstrates this convention (no interference by the opponents):

Opener	Responder
1x	1y
any but 1NT	2NT

Here *x* and *y* are suits, and 2NT is natural, and forcing for one round. Over 2NT, opener gets to make a third bid to complete the picture of his hand. Responder may pass a weak rebid:

Opener	Responder
1♦	1♠
2♠	2NT
3♠	pass

Opener	Responder
1♡	1♠
2♦	2NT
3♦	pass

If opener wants to make a forcing bid, he must bid 3♣, the fourth suit. On the other hand:

Opener	Responder
1♦	1♡
2♦	2NT
3♣	pass

Responder may pass this, because it's not the fourth suit.

Sequences responder may not pass:

Opener	Responder
1♦	1♡
2♣	2NT
3♦	

Opener	Responder
1♡	1♠
2♣	2NT
3♡	

These bids are forcing, because with a weak 6-4 opener should rebid the six immediately.

Opener	Responder
1♦	1♠
2♣	2NT
3♠	

This is forcing, because with 3-card support and a minimum, opener should raise to 2♠. If that happens, be aware of this sequence:

Opener	Responder
1♦	1♠
2♠	2NT
3♣	pass

This is not forcing, because it's not the fourth suit.

WHY USE NEW SUIT 2NT?

1) **You have the fourth suit well stopped and you want to declare the notrump contract.**

2) **You want to bid 2NT and later raise partner's suit to offer a choice of games.**

3) **You want to get 'real' information from your partner. Bidding the fourth suit doesn't obtain real information, because it forces opener into a corner:**

Opener	Responder
1♢	1♡
2♣	?

You hold as responder:

♠ A Q ♡ A J 10 7 4 ♢ K 6 3 ♣ J 10 5

If you bid 2♠ and partner bids 3♣, you have no idea what he has. He is forced to bid 3♣ with

♠ 5 2 ♡ Q 6 ♢ A J 8 7 4 ♣ A Q 3 2

because he has no spade stopper and no heart fit. But when you rebid 2NT, partner can bid naturally, raising to 3NT (on this example hand) or rebidding a suit to show a shapely hand (for example, a minimum 5-5) or rebidding 3♠ (fourth suit) to show a strong shapely hand.

4) **You can now use the jump to 3NT as a mild slam invitation, a hand with 16-17 points.**

Back to our preview:

♠ A 9 8 7 ♡ Q 8 7 5 ♢ K 2 ♣ A J 2

Partner opens 1♣. You respond 1♡. Partner rebids 2♣.

Partner	You
1♣	1♡
2♣	2NT

Over your Forcing 2NT, partner now bids 3♢. You bid 3♠ and partner bids 4♠! Are you prepared to bid a slam now? You can actually make 7♣. But at one table, the player with this hand bid 3NT over 2♣ and went down one.

```
                        ♠ K Q 3
                        ♡ —
                        ◊ A 6 5 4
                        ♣ K Q 10 8 7 6
    ♠ J 2                   ┌─────────┐              ♠ 10 6 5 4
    ♡ A J 9 4 3             │    N    │              ♡ K 10 6 2
    ◊ J 8 7              W  │         │  E           ◊ Q 10 9 3
    ♣ 5 4 3                 │    S    │              ♣ 9
                           └─────────┘
                        ♠ A 9 8 7
                        ♡ Q 8 7 5
                        ◊ K 2
                        ♣ A J 2
```

West	North	East	South
	1♣	pass	1♡
pass	2♣	pass	3NT
all pass			

West led the ♡4. East made a nice play by returning the ten, and that was that.
Using New Suit 2NT, the auction went:

North	South
1♣	1♡
2♣	2NT
3◊	3♠
4♠	6♣
pass	

This pair didn't have the 'machinery' to reach the grand slam, but the simple New Suit 2NT did enable them to reach six clubs, for a big gain.

The Law of Total Tricks Utility

A great deal has been written about the Law of Total Tricks. To review:
In competition, you have a close decision. You are not sure whether to bid one more or pass. To decide, you use the Law of Total Tricks.

1) *You guess the number of trumps between your side and the opponents' side and add them up. For example, suppose your side is bidding spades and they are bidding hearts. The auction is up to three hearts. Do you bid three spades? You calculate the likely number of spades between you and partner and the number of hearts between the opponents and add it all up. Say you get 18.*

2) *Then you calculate into the equation whether you have wasted honors — honors in their suit that are only good for defense. Then you adjust your total accordingly, subtracting for wasted honors, and adding for length in side suits. Let's say you still get 18.*

3) *You then apply the concept that the total number of trumps is equal to the total number of tricks for both sides. If they can make three hearts exactly, you can make three spades. If they are going one down, you can make an overtrick. If they can make an overtrick you are going one down.*

4) *You look at the vulnerability and decide what will happen to you if you bid. Then you take the appropriate action.*

It is actually a pretty good empirical method, and certainly gives better results than guessing. The rub is that the evaluation process is complicated. What if you are unable to make these calculations at the table quickly? You may bar your partner from making a bid even if you hesitate for only a few seconds and then pass. Because you must be able to make your competitive call in tempo, you must be adept at making your Law calculation before it is your turn to bid. Hence the advent of the Law Utility.

THE LAW UTILITY

Instead of adding up all the trumps, stick to your own trumps. But you don't even add these! You simply keep a tiny calculation of plus or minus in your head and for each number 'plus' you bid to one more level. Remember, of course, this only applies when you have a questionable decision.

Suppose you hold as West:

♠ A Q 7 5 4 2   ♡ Q 6   ◇ K J 3   ♣ 8 5

West	North	East	South
1♠	2♡	2♠	3♡
?			

When you hear LHO bid two hearts, you say to yourself ,'Minus 1' because of your wasted ♡Q. Partner raises to 2♠ so you calculate, 'One extra trump, add one, back to zero — I am not planning to bid again.' By the time South raises, only a few seconds later, you are ready to make a pass in tempo, so that your partner can ethically bid 3♠ if he wishes.

Let's change one card:

♠ A Q 7 5 4 2   ♡ Q 6   ◇ K J 3 2   ♣ 5

West	North	East	South
1♠	2♡	2♠	3♡
?			

Now when you hear 2♠ from partner, you say to yourself, 'One extra trump and one extra diamond, minus one wasted honor in hearts for a total of +1 — I will bid again.'

Let's change a different card:

♠ A Q 7 5 4 2   ♡ 7 6   ◇ K Q J   ♣ 8 5

West	North	East	South
1♠	2♡	2♠	3♡
?			

Quick calculation: 'No wastage, one extra trump — bid one more.'

Let's move a club into the diamond suit:

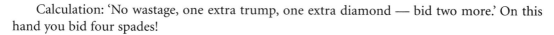

♠ A Q 7 5 4 2 ♡ 7 6 ◇ K Q J 5 ♣ 8

West	North	East	South
1♠	2♡	2♠	3♡
?			

Calculation: 'No wastage, one extra trump, one extra diamond — bid two more.' On this hand you bid four spades!

The 10-12 Notrump

This convention was introduced decades ago as part of the EHAA system (EHAA stands for 'Every Hand An Adventure'). Over the years, it has gained credibility and is now used by many strong pairs.

Be careful: if you use 1NT to show 10-12, you must agree with partner about how to show 13-15 and 16-18 ranges. The easiest solution is to rebid 1NT after a minor-suit opening bid with 13-16, scale down the 2NT jump rebid to show 17 to a bad 19, and open 2NT with a good 19-20.

Most people do not use the 10-12 notrump at all vulnerabilities. Some use it only at favorable vulnerability, and some use it when not vulnerable in first and second seat only.

Here's the complete system:

Opener	Responder
1NT (10-12)	?
2♣	nonforcing Stayman
2♢	forcing Stayman
2♡	to play
2♠	to play
2NT	forces 3♣, many types of hands (see below)
3♣	slightly invitational
3♢	slightly invitational
3♡	preemptive
3♠	preemptive

Here are the auctions after the 2NT relay:

Opener	Responder
1NT	2NT
3♣	?
pass	clubs
3♢	signoff in diamonds
3♡	5-5 majors, invitational
3♠	short spades
3NT	short hearts

ESCAPING THE AXE

The big danger occurs when the 10-12 is doubled. Most pairs play a special runout method such as the following:

Opener	Oppt	Responder
1NT	dbl	?
	redbl	two suits (4-4 at least), touching
	pass	two suits not touching or a desire to play 1NT redoubled; opener must redouble and responder passes or bids the lower of his two non-touching suits
	2 suit	to play, presumably a one-suited hand

AN UNADVERTISED PLUS

Not only does the 10-12 notrump obstruct the opponents bidding (by taking up the entire one-level), but you can sometimes get them for a number after a 10-12 notrump opening! Here's an illustration from world championship play (the 1994 Venice Cup). The American West was Jill Meyers and East, Kay Schulle. Neither side was vulnerable.

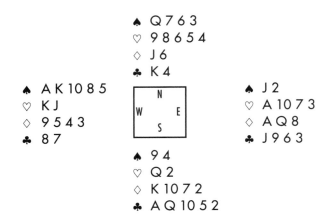

```
              ♠ Q 7 6 3
              ♡ 9 8 6 5 4
              ◇ J 6
              ♣ K 4
♠ A K 10 8 5      ┌─────────┐      ♠ J 2
♡ K J             │    N    │      ♡ A 10 7 3
◇ 9 5 4 3         │ W     E │      ◇ A Q 8
♣ 8 7             │    S    │      ♣ J 9 6 3
                  └─────────┘
              ♠ 9 4
              ♡ Q 2
              ◇ K 10 7 2
              ♣ A Q 10 5 2
```

West	North	East	South
		1NT	pass
2♠	pass	pass	2NT
dbl	pass	pass	3♣
pass	pass	dbl	all pass

Can you blame South for balancing? The result was six tricks for South, down three, minus 500. Notice that East-West had already won this board by stopping in two spades, warned by the 10-12 opening that game was unlikely. The 500 number was icing on the cake!

Fine Arts Conventions

Trent Weak Two-Bids – A Treatise

The Trent weak two-bid* is a version of regular weak two-bids in which the emphasis is not on preempting the opponents. Here are the guidelines:

1) The Trent weak two-bid shows a good playing hand (7-12 high card points); the idea is to get into the auction and compete to the best partscore or game.
2) The Trent weak two-bid shows at least a trick on defense. If you have a hand with a long suit and no aces or kings, open at the three-level or pass.
3) The Trent weak two-bid requires a six-card suit (except in third seat), but aside from that you can have any distribution. You can have a seven-card suit. You can be six-five. You can certainly be six-four.
4) After opening a Trent weak two-bid, you can bid again. With the correct shape, you can compete later in the auction by making a takeout double, rebidding your suit (with a 7-bagger), or bidding a new suit.

---

*   Based on the weak two-bids played by Paul and Sandy Trent, advocated by us for many years, and regularly used with great success by pairs such as Zia Mahmood and Michael Rosenberg

With neither side vulnerable, you, West, hold:

♠ K J 7 2   ♡ K Q 9 6 5 4   ◇ 9   ♣ J 6

West	North	East	South
?			

If you would pass because you don't open a weak two-bid with four cards in the other major, take a look at this deal from OKbridge:

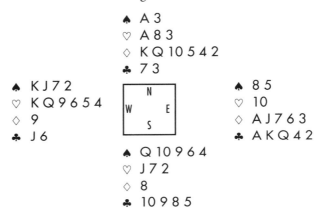

	♠ A 3	
	♡ A 8 3	
	◇ K Q 10 5 4 2	
	♣ 7 3	

♠ K J 7 2   ♠ 8 5
♡ K Q 9 6 5 4   ♡ 10
◇ 9   ◇ A J 7 6 3
♣ J 6   ♣ A K Q 4 2

♠ Q 10 9 6 4
♡ J 7 2
◇ 8
♣ 10 9 8 5

West	North	East	South
2♡	3◇	dbl	all pass

The result: 1100 to East-West.

Here's another example:

Opener	Responder
♠ Q 10 8 2	♠ 7
♡ 5 4	♡ A 10 2
◇ K Q J 5 4 2	◇ A 10 8 7
♣ 8	♣ A K Q 9 4
2◇	4♣[1]
4♡[2]	6◇

1. Keycard Gerber for diamonds.
2. One keycard.

Try getting to this slam if the dealer, too squeamish to open a weak two diamonds with a four-card major, passes.

WHEN NOT TO USE A TRENT WEAK TWO-BID

You should *not* open a Trent weak two-bid with any of these hands:

a) too weak a suit

♠ J 8 6 5 3 2   ♡ A K Q 4   ◇ 8 2   ♣ 3

Using common sense, you do not open 2♠ with such a weak suit. You do not want a spade lead against any contract. You are strong enough to compete later.

b) too strong a suit

♠ K Q J 10 9 8   ♡ 9   ◇ A J 8 2   ♣ 8 3

This time your suit is strong enough to play opposite shortness. You do not want to put partner under pressure if he happens to have a good hand and short spades. For example, suppose partner holds:

♠ 3   ♡ A K 5 2   ◇ K 10 4 3   ♣ A 5 4 2

He will pass your opening two spades and hope they balance. Meanwhile, the diamond slam is on a finesse.

Instead, with a one-loser suit and 11-12 high card points, open this kind of hand at the one-level.

c) a weak diamond suit

♠ A J 3   ♡ 5   ◇ J 8 7 5 3 2   ♣ K J 10

One of the objectives in opening a weak two-diamond bid is to get to three notrump. If your diamond suit is as weak as this one, there is no point in opening.

WHEN TO USE A TRENT WEAK TWO-BID

In contrast, do open these hands with a Trent weak two-bid:

a) a hand too good to preempt

♠ A Q 10 9 8 7 2   ♡ 8   ◇ Q J 3 2   ♣ 9

This hand is much too good to open with three spades. You want to convey to partner that you have a very good playing hand. Most players today do this by opening this hand at the one-level, but what does this do for you? It's highly possible that the opponents will compete in hearts or clubs, and you will be forced to rebid your spades at whatever level necessary, and how will partner know whether you have this sort of hand or a much stronger hand? Would you be surprised if the auction went:

You	Oppt	Partner	Oppt
1♠	2♠[1]	dbl	4♡

1. Michaels.

In contrast, when you open two spades and later bid four spades, partner knows you have less than 13 points and will be able to make a good competitive decision accordingly.

b) a hand with a good second suit

♠ K J 10 7 6 3   ♡ 8   ◇ A Q 10 3 2   ♣ 7

Open two spades. Later you will bid your diamonds. Here again, if you open at the one-level, it's not going to be so easy to bid your second suit. Partner might think you have a big hand! Playing Trent weak two-bids, the whole auction went:

You	Oppt	Partner	Oppt
2♠	3♣	dbl[1]	pass
3◇	pass	4NT	pass
5◇	pass	6◇	all pass

1. Penalty.

```
                      ♠ Q
                      ♡ A 9 7
                      ◇ K J 9 8
                      ♣ A J 9 4 3
     ♠ A 2                              ♠ 9 8 5 4
     ♡ K Q J 3        ┌─────┐           ♡ 10 6 5 4 2
     ◇ 5            W │  N  │ E         ◇ 7 6 4
     ♣ K Q 10 8 6 5   │  S  │           ♣ 2
                      └─────┘
                      ♠ K J 10 7 6 3
                      ♡ 8
                      ◇ A Q 10 3 2
                      ♣ 7
```

North knew his partner was six-five because otherwise he would not have pulled the penalty double. The hand was an open book and North had an easy slam bid.

c) the classic hand

♠ Q J 10 8 5 3   ♡ ——   ◇ A K 9 3   ♣ J 5 2

Here again, most people would open with one spade, thinking that the hand is too good for a weak two-bid (first round controls in two outside suits? An ace-king on the side? Oh my gosh!!!). And it is, unless you're playing the Trent version. Now you can open 2♠. You can compete later with a takeout double. And again, having limited your hand, you can bid your head off for the rest of the auction.

Here's another real-life deal, this time from the Spingold Knockout Teams.

You are in first seat, not vulnerable against vulnerable:

♠ A Q J 8 5 4　♡ 5　◇ J 9 3　♣ Q 7 4

West	North	East	South
		2♠	3♡
pass	pass	?	

What would you do?

Matthew (North) was hoist by his own petard when playing against Zia (East), because Zia (playing Trent weak twos) doubled. At the other table, the East player also opened two spades, but did not double in the passout seat. After Zia's double, it went all pass. The entire deal was:

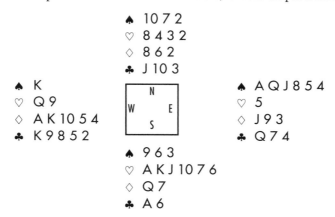

East-West took three spades, two diamonds and a club, for down two and plus 500.

RESPONSES TO THE TRENT WEAK TWO-BID

East-West are vulnerable. You are North and hold:

♠ A 7　♡ K Q 3 2　◇ A 9 5　♣ A K 5 2

West	North	East	South
			2♡
pass	?		

In the past, North would have been content to bid game. After all, a favorable vulnerability weak two-bid rated to be extremely weak. And, even if partner had a maximum, how could you find out if he had the right cards or right shape? Nowadays, the power of the Trent weak two-bid allows everyone to have the appropriate 'machinery' for investigating slams. This deal is from the USA Team Trials for the World Olympiad Teams; it helped Larry Cohen and David Berkowitz win a big swing, and their team went on to win the Trials. (The hand has been rotated to make South the declarer.)

East-West vul.

	♠ A 7	
	♡ K Q 3 2	
	◇ A 9 5	
	♣ A K 5 2	
♠ 10 4 3 2		♠ K Q J 9 6 5
♡ 10 5		♡ 9
◇ K 7 3 2		◇ J 10 8 4
♣ 9 6 3		♣ J 10
	♠ 8	
	♡ A J 8 7 6 4	
	◇ Q 6	
	♣ Q 8 7 4	

West	North	East	South
	Cohen		Berkowitz
			2♡
pass	2NT	pass	3♣[1]
pass	4♣[2]	pass	4♡[3]
pass	5NT[4]	pass	6♣
pass	7♣	all pass	

1. Club feature (ace, king or queen).
2. Keycard Blackwood for hearts.
3. One keycard.
4. Pick a slam.

When Berkowitz bid 6♣, he indicated four of them, so Cohen was able to bid the grand slam, knowing that his partner must have a singleton somewhere. And wherever his partner had that singleton (in spades or diamonds), he would able to take a ruff in hand for an extra trick in a club contract. Seven clubs scored 1440. At the other table, North-South stopped in 6♡ making six, 980, for a swing of 460 points to the Cohen-Berkowitz team.

Here's the recommended response structure (specific examples follow below):

1) **A new suit is constructive but not forcing.**

   If opener does not like his partner's suit and he does not like his hand, he can pass. He can raise, rebid his suit, or bid a new suit with the appropriate hand. To force, responder must start with 2NT.

2) **2NT is forcing and asks partner to describe his hand. The rebids by opener are:**

A new suit at the three-level is natural, showing a four-card suit (this is different from the way Berkowitz-Cohen play their responses);

A new suit at the four-level is natural, and shows a five-card suit;

A jump to game in the weak-two suit shows a seven-card suit;

3NT shows a good suit and a good hand (with no side suit);

Simple rebid of opener's suit is a catchall — none of the above.

A new suit by responder after opener's rebid is natural and forcing, for example:

Opener	Responder
2♠	2NT
3♣[1]	3♡[2]

1. Four-card club suit.
2. Natural, forcing.

3) **4♣ is Keycard Gerber for opener's suit.**

4) **4NT is plain Blackwood.**

5) **A suit at the five-level is Exclusion Keycard Blackwood.**

6) **A simple raise is non-invitational and can be made with a doubleton.** It can also be made with a weak hand. Opener can raise himself to game if he likes.

7) **After a 2♡ or 2♠ opening bid, 4♢ is a slam try with ace, king or queen doubleton of trumps.**

Let's look at some of these auctions in a little more detail, with illustrations:

1. A new suit is constructive but not forcing.

Suppose the auction goes:

Opener	Responder
2♡	2♠
?	

The rebids are:

Pass	**nowhere to go**
2NT	**natural, not forcing**
3♣	**natural, four+ card suit (or strong fragment, looking for notrump) forcing**
3♢	**natural, four+ card suit (or strong fragment, looking for notrump), forcing**
3♡	**natural, good suit (can play opposite shortness), not forcing**
3♠	**raise, not forcing**
4♣	**singleton or void, 4+ spades (denies great controls)**
4♢	**singleton or void, 4+ spades (denies great controls)**
4♡	**natural, 7-card suit (exceptional)**
4♠	**maximum raise, 3-card support**
3NT	**super-dooper maximum raise, four-card support plus good controls**

Opener	Responder
♠ 5	♠ A K J 9 8
♡ A 10 8 7 3 2	♡ 4
♢ A 9 4	♢ K Q 10
♣ 10 5 2	♣ J 9 7 3

2♡	2♠
pass[1]	

1. No spade fit, minimum hand; nothing to say.

Opener	**Responder**
♠ 10 5 2	♠ A K J 9 8
♡ A 10 8 7 3 2	♡ 4
◇ A 9 4	◇ K Q 10
♣ 5	♣ J 9 7 3

2♡	2♠
3♠[1]	4♠[2]

1. Non-forcing spade raise.
2. Even if opener's minors are reversed, game is not terrible.

Opener	**Responder**
♠ Q 10 5 2	♠ A K J 9 8
♡ K J 8 7 3 2	♡ 4
◇ A 9	◇ K Q 10
♣ 5	♣ J 9 7 3

2♡	2♠
4♣[1]	4♠[2]

1. Singleton club, four trumps, denies great controls.
2. Missing three aces so he knows there's no slam.

Opener	**Responder**
♠ Q 10 5 2	♠ A K J 9 8
♡ A 10 8 7 3 2	♡ 4
◇ A 9	◇ K Q 10
♣ 5	♣ J 9 7 3

2♡	2♠
3NT[1]	4◇[2]
4NT[3]	5♡
6♠	

1. Super-dooper raise; four trumps plus controls.
2. Cuebid, denies a club control.
3. Sounds like partner's worried about clubs; I've got clubs under control so I'll bid Keycard Blackwood.

2. 2NT is forcing and asks partner to describe his hand.

See the response chart above. Here's a typical auction:

Opener	Responder
♠ A K J 10 3 2	♠ Q 9 4
♡ K 5 2	♡ A 8 3
◇ 8 3	◇ A 9 4
♣ 7 6	♣ A 5 4 2

2♠	2NT
3NT	pass

Responder was on the way to four spades, but stops in three notrump for all the match-points.

3. 4♣ is Keycard Gerber for opener's suit.

Opener	Responder
♠ K J 9 5 4 2	♠ A 3
♡ 9 8	♡ K Q 4 2
◇ 10 4	◇ A K Q J 6 2
♣ K Q 3	♣ 9

2♠	4♣
4♡[1]	4♠[2]

1. One or four keycards.
2. Whoops, let's stop right here.

4. 4NT is plain Blackwood.

Opener	Responder
♠ A Q 9 8 4 2	♠ 3
♡ 9 8 2	♡ A K
◇ K 4 3	◇ A 5
♣ 7	♣ A K Q J 10 9 3 2

2♠	4NT
5◇	5NT
6◇	7NT

Not an easy hand to bid if responder cannot simply ask for aces!

5. A suit at the five-level is Exclusion Keycard Blackwood.

Opener	Responder
♠ Q J 10 5 4 2	♠ A K 9 8
♡ A 5	♡ K Q J 3
◇ Q 4 2	◇ —
♣ 8 3	♣ K Q J 10 9

2♠	5◇
5♠[1]	6♠

1. One keycard outside diamonds.

6. A simple raise is non-invitational.

Opener	Responder
♠ A K 10 8 3 2	♠ Q 4
♡ 8	♡ A 9 4
◇ Q J 10 4 2	◇ K 5 3
♣ 6	♣ 9 8 4 3 2

2♠	3♠
4♠[1]	

1. Opener, with a maximum and great playing strength, is entitled to bid again.

7. After a 2♡ or 2♠ opening bid, 4◇ is a slam try with ace, king or queen doubleton trumps.

This agreement allows for slam exploration while at the same time making sure that the trump fit is solid enough to play at the six-level.

Opener	Responder
♠ A Q 10 8 3 2	♠ K 4
♡ K 9 3	♡ A Q 7 4
◇ 10 4	◇ A K 9 2
♣ 6 3	♣ A 4 2

2♠	4◇
4♡ [1]	4NT [2]
5◇ [3]	5♡ [4]
6♡ [5]	6♠

1. Cuebid – confirms that the trump suit is fine.
2. Keycard Blackwood.
3. One keycard.
4. Trump queen?
5. Yes, plus the ♡K (but no ♣K).

Opener	Responder
♠ A Q J 8 3 2	♠ K 4
♡ 8	♡ A 9 4
◇ Q J 10 4	◇ A 9 3
♣ 6 5	♣ A K Q 9 4

2♠	4◇
4♡ [1]	4NT [2]
5◇ [3]	5♡ [4]
5NT [5]	6♠

1. Cuebid – confirms that the trump suit is fine.
2. Keycard Blackwood.
3. One keycard.
4. Trump queen?
5. Yes, but no kings.

Opener	Responder
♠ J 10 7 5 3 2	♠ K 4
♡ K 9	♡ A 9 4
◇ K Q 2	◇ A 9 3
♣ J 6	♣ A K Q 9 4

2♠	4◇
4♠[1]	pass

1. Forget it, trumps aren't good enough to play opposite honor doubleton.

Let's go back to the Cohen-Berkowitz hand (page 244). How would you bid it using our response system? Here's our recommended auction:

Opener	Responder
♠ 8	♠ A 7
♡ A J 8 7 6 4	♡ K Q 3 2
◇ Q 6	◇ A 9 5
♣ Q 8 7 4	♣ A K 5 2

2♡	2NT
3♣[1]	4♣[2]
4♡[3]	4NT[4]
5◇[5]	5♠[6]
7♣[7]	

1. Natural, four-card suit.
2. Natural, forcing.
3. Cuebid.
4. Keycard Blackwood for clubs, the only suit bid and raised.
5. One or four keycards.
6. Queen-Ask.
7. Got it.

Here's another wild hand that works well with these methods. You hold

♠ A 10 7 3　♡ 9　♢ A K 8 5 3 2　♣ A 10

and partner opens 2♡ in first seat. A simple 3♢ by you would not be forcing, so you bid 2NT.

Partner	You
2♡	2NT
4♢[1]	4NT[2]
5♢	7♢

1. This is a strange development — partner has five diamonds and six hearts!
2. Plain Blackwood because your 2NT bid didn't promise heart support and you have no room to raise diamonds and then use Keycard.

Here are the two hands:

♠ A 10 7 3　♡ 9　♢ A K 8 5 3 2　♣ A 10

♠ —　♡ A 8 7 6 4 3　♢ Q J 10 9　♣ 4 3 2

THE TRENT WEAK TWO-BID IN COMPETITION

What happens after we open a Trent weak two-bid and they make a takeout double? East-West are vulnerable, and you, North, hold:

♠ A J 8 4　♡ 7　♢ K Q J 3 2　♣ Q 8 2

West	North	East	South
			2♡
dbl	?		

The responses are:

Redouble	**it's our hand; either we play it or they play it doubled**
2NT	**game try in opener's suit**
New suit (non-jump) or raise	**to play**
Jump shift	**lead director plus fit**
Pass and later double	**penalty**

In this case, North redoubles. The auction continues:

West	North	East	South
			2♡
dbl	redbl	pass	pass
3♣	dbl[1]	all pass	

1. Important Principle: If your side is in a 'let's get 'em' auction, a double by either partner does not promise a 'stack' — it shows three cards in the suit bid plus a good defensive hand. If you have a 'stack' in each of the other three suits, pass the takeout double for now, rather than redoubling; you will later double them and that later double shows a stack.

The whole deal:

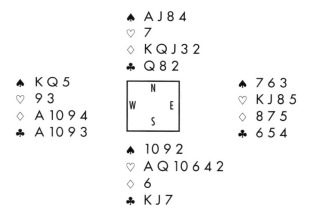

Poor East-West. When the smoke cleared they were -1400.

South does not have to sit for the penalty double with a singleton. Suppose instead he has:

♠ 9 5 2   ♡ Q J 10 9 8 3   ◇ A 10 4   ♣ 7

Now he has only one trick on defense and a singleton in their suit. If he pulls to 3♡ and they were going for a number, he need not apologize; better safe than sorry. The whole deal in this case might be:

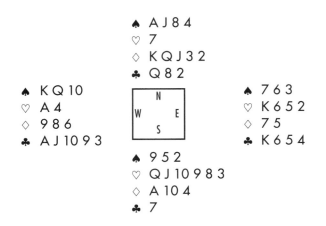

	♠ A J 8 4
	♡ 7
	◇ K Q J 3 2
	♣ Q 8 2

♠ K Q 10		♠ 7 6 3
♡ A 4		♡ K 6 5 2
◇ 9 8 6		◇ 7 5
♣ A J 10 9 3		♣ K 6 5 4

	♠ 9 5 2
	♡ Q J 10 9 8 3
	◇ A 10 4
	♣ 7

West	North	East	South
			2♡
dbl	redbl	pass	pass
3♣	dbl	pass	3♡[1]
all pass			

1. Not every Trent weak two-bid is a maximum. A measure of cooperation is necessary to play these bids successfully, just as it is after an opening one-bid.

Result: making three.

As mentioned above, if North had a trump stack in every suit, he would pass over the take-out double and later double for penalties, without looking for cooperation.

After they double the weak two-bid, a new suit is to play. For example:

West	North	East	South
			2♡
dbl	3♣		

North has something like:

♠ 10 5 4   ♡ —   ◇ A 7 3   ♣ Q J 10 9 8 3 2

A jump-shift, however, shows a fit for opener's suit, plus strength in the suit bid:

West	North	East	South
			2♡
dbl	4♣		

North has something like:

♠ 10 5 4   ♡ Q 10 8   ◇ 9 2   ♣ A K Q 10 4

Here North is willing to compete to four hearts, but if East bids something, he wants to make sure partner leads a club, not a heart.

TRENT WEAK JUMP OVERCALLS

The same principles that underly the Trent weak two-bid philosophy can be applied successfully to 'weak' jump overcalls. Here's a real-life example from the 2000 Cavendish Invitational Teams.

With both sides vulnerable, you hold as West:

♠ 5   ♡ A J 10 7 6 2   ◇ 10 7 4   ♣ A J 6

West	North	East	South
			1◇
?			

What is your call?

This hand was reported in the ACBL *Bridge Bulletin* (August 2000). The world champion who held this hand bid one heart. The hand did not develop nicely for him:

West	North	East	South
			1◇
1♡	2◇	2♠[1]	2NT
pass	3NT	pass	pass
?			

1. Not forcing.

Now West doubled. What would you lead?

West led the ♡10 and finished up -950. Amazingly, this result was duplicated at several other tables. The whole deal was:

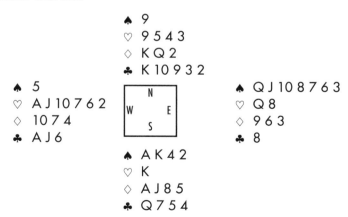

A low heart is the winner, but probably zero out of 1000 expert bridge players would make that lead on this auction. West probably considered the ♡10 or his singleton spade. In either case, if declarer guesses clubs (which he did), he makes his contract.

Would declarer have guessed the clubs after a Trent weak jump overcall? We think not. In addition, it's not clear who would end up declaring this hand. What would North do after:

West	North	East	South
			1♢
2♡	?		

North is stuck and will probably pass for now, waiting for his partner's reopening double. But the auction continues:

West	North	East	South
			1♢
2♡	pass	3♡	?

South knows that his partner doesn't have four spades (or if he does he has a very weak hand), so what is South supposed to do? He probably passes. North knows his opponents have at least eight spades so despite his nine points, he may decide to pass as well, and East-West will play the hand in 3♡! They'll finish down one or two, a far better result (even if North or South manages to find a double) than -950.

The Trent weak two-bid, then, can also be played in competition. If you're favorable and have a horrible hand, pass or overcall at the three-level. For example, if they are vulnerable and you are not, holding

♠ A J 10 8 3 2   ♡ 8 4 2   ♢ A J 8   ♣ 4

bid a bold 2♠ over a 1♡ opening. But with

♠ Q J 10 8 3 2   ♡ 8 4 2   ♢ Q 8 4   ♣ 4

summon up your courage and overcall 3♠.

However, suppose you have:

♠ K Q J 10 8 2   ♡ 8 4 2   ♢ A J 8   ♣ 4

Now your right call is 1♠ if RHO opens 1♡. Just as you don't open a Trent weak two-bid with a one-loser suit, don't jump overcall with one either. You can easily have a 4♠ or 3NT game, and do not want to put undue pressure on partner should he hold something like:

♠ 2   ♡ A Q 4   ♢ K 7 6 2   ♣ A J 9 4 2

He wouldn't dream of bidding after a 2♠ overcall by you (nor should he), yet 3NT is just about 'on ice'.

After the Trent jump overcall, the responses are basically the same as they were over the opening weak two-bid, except now there is an additional tool, a cuebid of their suit.

Situation #1

Oppt	Partner	Oppt	You
1♢	2♡	pass	3♢

Situation #2

Oppt	Partner	Oppt	You
1♢	2♡	pass	2NT[1]

1. Forcing.

The 2NT bid in the second situation is no longer likely to be made with a big fit in hearts. The cuebid is a game try in partner's suit; the 2NT bid, then, shows a hand either with a strong suit of its own or interest in playing 3NT. If the overcaller is minimum, he rebids his suit.

Suppose the 2♡ overcaller has:

♠ 10 8 3   ♡ A Q J 10 4 3   ♢ Q 8   ♣ 8 7

If his partner bids 3♢, he signs off in 3♡. He's got a nice suit, but poor distribution and altogether nothing to write home about (if his queen of diamonds — their suit — were the queen of clubs or spades, his hand would be much better). The whole deal was:

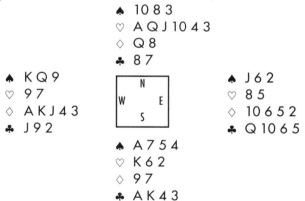

```
                 ♠ 10 8 3
                 ♡ A Q J 10 4 3
                 ♢ Q 8
                 ♣ 8 7
  ♠ K Q 9                        ♠ J 6 2
  ♡ 9 7          N               ♡ 8 5
  ♢ A K J 4 3  W   E             ♢ 10 6 5 2
  ♣ J 9 2          S             ♣ Q 10 6 5
                 ♠ A 7 5 4
                 ♡ K 6 2
                 ♢ 9 7
                 ♣ A K 4 3
```

West	North	East	South
1♢	2♡	pass	3♢
pass	3♡	all pass	

If partner bids 2NT, however, the overcaller should take a shot at 3NT. His heart suit might be good for six tricks, his queen of diamonds is a much better card now, and his poor distribution isn't such a detriment. The whole deal might be:

♠ 10 8 3
♡ A Q J 10 4 3
◇ Q 8
♣ 8 7

♠ K Q 7   ♠ 6 5 4 2
♡ 9 8 2   ♡ 7 6
◇ A K 6 3 2   ◇ 7 5
♣ J 9   ♣ K 10 6 5 2

♠ A J 9
♡ K 5
◇ J 10 9 4
♣ A Q 4 3

West	North	East	South
1◇	2♡	pass	2NT
pass	3NT	all pass	

Suppose South has a suit of his own:

North
♠ 10 8 3
♡ A Q J 10 4 3
◇ Q 8
♣ 8 7

South
♠ A K 4
♡ 8
◇ J 3 2
♣ A K Q J 5 3

West	North	East	South
1◇	2♡	pass	2NT
pass	3NT	pass	?

South has no reason to introduce his club suit. He's got eight tricks in his own hand and North has denied a second suit, so probably has at least two diamonds (and hence there's probably no slam). South has to hope for the best, and this time he's lucky.

Suppose North's spades and diamonds are reversed. North-South will need diamonds to break 4-3 or have the suit block, but they are nevertheless in the best game since 5♣ has no play (and 4♡ virtually none) after a diamond lead.

ONE FINAL WRINKLE

Oppt	Partner	Oppt	You
1♢	2♡	pass	4♣ or 4♢

Jump shifts to the four-level in the minor suits are splinter bids. They are not lead-directing-with-a-fit bids, because this time we have no reason to think the opponents will be playing the hand (which was more likely after a takeout double, where one opponent is known to have a good playing hand with shortness in our suit).

The Trump Cuebid

In the bidding, there are situations where you want to 'show and tell' and there are other situations where you need to obtain some information from partner.

Suppose the bidding goes:

You	Partner
1♠	2◇[1]
2♠	?

1. Game-forcing.

What is the difference between bidding three spades and four spades here? (Assume both bids are forcing.)

Many people play that four spades is a shutout bid, that is, 'I have no interest in slam.' A better way to play the unnecessary jump is, 'In the context of the bidding, I have great trump support!'

Suppose on the above auction the two hands are:

Opener	Responder
♠ A 10 8 6 5 2	♠ K Q 9
♡ A	♡ 10 7 3
◇ Q 4	◇ A K J 5 2
♣ K 8 4 2	♣ Q 3

Playing the unnecessary jump to four spades as a **Trump Cuebid**, the auction continues:

Opener	Responder
1♠	2◇[1]
2♠	4♠[2]
4NT	5♠[3]
6♠	

1. Game-forcing.
2. Great trumps.
3. Two keycards plus the trump queen.

The opener has a very strong hand once he knows his partner has strong three-card trump support. In addition, the trump cuebid implies nothing else to cuebid (you don't want to suppress an important control, so you don't jump to game on hands that contain are). Therefore, the opener can just about take it to the bank that his partner has good spades and good diamonds.

Suppose instead the two hands were:

Opener	Responder
♠ A 10 8 6 5 2	♠ K Q 9
♡ Q 4	♡ A 2
◇ A	◇ K Q J 8 3
♣ K 8 4 2	♣ 7 5 3

1♠	2◇
2♠	3♠[1]
4♣	4NT
5♡	6♠

1. Responder's three-spade raise is defined as a minimum raise or a slam try, looking for controls.

Responder does not jump to four spades, despite holding strong trumps, because this time he does not want to 'show and tell' — he wants to find out if his partner has a club control.

Another example:

Opener	Responder
♠ A K Q	♠ J 10 8 7 5 2
♡ 10 8 2	♡ Q
◇ A Q 6	◇ K 9 5
♣ A 9 7 2	♣ K Q 3

The bidding should go:

Opener	Responder
1♣	1♠
2◇	2♠
4♠	4NT
etc.	

East finds out that his partner has enough keycards for slam and duly bids it. This hand is going to be very clumsy to bid if West's trump holding can be anything from ace-king-queen to king-third or even queen-third. The trump cuebid makes everything easy.

Word of caution: do not show and tell if you can take control of the auction instead. This is a mistake frequently made when first using the trump cuebid. Players jump to game with strong trumps, but partner has no bid. Here's an example that appeared in *Bridge Today* magazine (March/April 1995 issue):

Bridge is not always a partnership game by Alvin Roth

Let me give you a hand from way back. I was giving a lecture to advanced players (in D.C.) when I got a phone call from a friend in Miami who was upset over the following (IMPs, both vul):

♠ Q J 3   ♡ A K Q 6   ◇ 5   ♣ K 8 7 6 4

Partner opens one spade; you bid two clubs. Partner bids two hearts. Now what?

I answered that there is no way I could describe this hand. Therefore, I had to bid single-handedly. I would use Blackwood, and if partner showed three aces, I would bid 5NT. If he showed a king, I would bid seven. On the actual hand, partner showed two aces, so I would bid six hearts.

When I asked my friend what gives, she stated I missed seven. This did not surprise me, for I knew we might miss seven if partner were void in clubs, which was the case. But there was one more punch line. Why was she so disturbed, I asked. What did she do? She said that she jumped to four hearts to show strong trumps but partner passed with:

♠ A K 7 6 4   ♡ J 9 7 5 2   ◇ A 6 3   ♣ —

Perhaps partner should bid 5◇ over 4♠, but he can't really be blamed for passing.

What is the lesson? Not that responder must splinter or use Keycard Blackwood or other such nonsense. The lesson is more practical: the player who sees a slam and cannot possibly describe his hand must take the bull by the horns and drive to that slam, knowing that a grand slam might be missed. I've never been afraid of missing a grand slam, for many times a player will bid a grand down one in a team event to find to his dismay that the other side was in game.

The Singleton Cuebid

Vulnerable against not, you pick up:

♠ 5   ♡ K 3   ◇ K 8 7 6 5 4   ♣ 10 9 7 6

Oppt	You	Oppt	Partner
pass	pass	2♠	dbl
pass	3◇	pass	3NT
pass	?		

Your hand wasn't much before, but it is now. You are a passed hand and made a weak bid over partner's takeout double, so you have shown nothing at all, whereas you have a potentially huge hand.

On the other hand, you aren't strong enough to go anywhere by yourself. Your diamond spots are weak, and you have no guarantee that partner has a diamond fit with you. Although a takeout double normally promises three cards in the unbid suits, this is not necessarily so when the doubler has a huge hand. Partner could have something like:

♠ A Q 5   ♡ A Q 8 7   ◇ A 3   ♣ K Q J 3

You have enough for him to make three notrump with an overtrick, but you have no play for six diamonds, and might even go down in five diamonds. Meanwhile, five or even six clubs may also be cold.

Then again, partner doesn't deny a three- or even four-card diamond fit. Suppose he has:

♠ A 10 5   ♡ A Q 8 7   ◇ A Q 3 2   ♣ A 3

What do you do over his 3NT bid, if anything?

THE SOLUTION

Is there any way you can make a little move, without propelling yourself into a no-play slam? Yes! The **Singleton Cuebid**.

You bid four spades over three notrump. This says, 'Partner, I have a singleton spade. I have the maximum for my previous bidding, and it's possible that we have a slam in diamonds, or perhaps in clubs (I have denied hearts).'

If opener rebids 4NT, you pass and play it there.

In real life, the whole deal was:

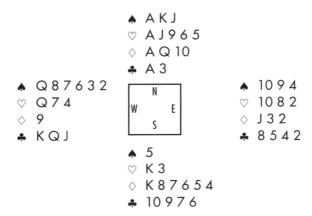

Oppt	You	Oppt	Partner
pass	pass	2♠	dbl
pass	3◇	pass	3NT
pass	4♠	pass	6◇
all pass			

Result: +1390, six diamonds making seven.

Here's a more common situation:

Oppt	You	Oppt	Partner
1♣	1NT	pass	2♡[1]
pass	2♠	pass	3♣

1. Transfer to spades.

You have:

♠ K 4   ♡ A K 8 4   ◇ Q J 8 4   ♣ A 10 8

Partner showed a singleton club, so three notrump is not the contract you want to play. Partner denied four hearts (no Stayman), so he rates to be 5-3-4-1. Here are four possible hands for his bidding — they all produce a slam!

Hand 1

♠ A Q J 8 2	♠ K 4
♡ 7 6 2	♡ A K 8 4
◇ K 10 3 2	◇ Q J 8 4
♣ 3	♣ A 10 8

Hand 2

♠ A 7 6 3 2	♠ K 4
♡ 7 6 2	♡ A K 8 4
◇ A K 3 2	◇ Q J 8 4
♣ 3	♣ A 10 8

Hand 3

♠ A 7 6 3 2	♠ K 4
♡ Q J 3	♡ A K 8 4
◇ A 9 3 2	◇ Q J 8 4
♣ 3	♣ A 10 8

Hand 4

♠ Q J 10 3 2	♠ K 4
♡ Q J 3	♡ A K 8 4
◇ A K 3 2	◇ Q J 8 4
♣ 3	♣ A 10 8

You make 6◇ opposite all four of these dummies!

Here's another situation where the singleton cuebid might come up. You have:

♠ 8 ♡ A 4 3 2 ◇ K 7 ♣ K Q J 5 4 2

You	Oppt	Partner	Oppt
1♣	1♠	2NT	pass
3♠			

You know your partner doesn't have four hearts, but this hand might still belong somewhere else besides notrump. With

♠ A J 3 ♡ K 7 ◇ A 9 8 2 ♣ 10 9 8 7

for example, partner will bid 4♣, and your side can get to six clubs, which is laydown (while 3NT goes down on a bad day).

Here's a final great example:

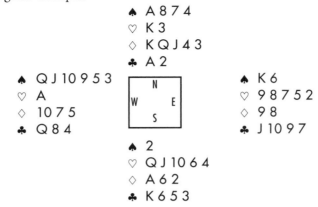

West	Partner	East	You
2♠	2NT	pass	3◇[1]
pass	3♡	pass	3♠[2]
pass	4NT	pass	5◇
pass	6◇!	all pass	

1. Transfer.
2. Singleton spade.

So here you are in a comfortably making slam. Meanwhile, in the other room they play 3NT, down one after the king of spades lead!

The Zia Cuebid

61

You hold:

♠ Q J   ♡ A K 8   ◇ A Q J 8 5 3   ♣ Q 5

Partner	You
1♠	2◇[1]
2♠	?

1. Game-forcing.

What now?

THE SOLUTION

There are many different hands partner can hold where slam is just about cold. For example:

Hand 1

♠ A K 10 3 2	♠ Q J
♡ J 4	♡ A K 8
◇ 6 2	◇ A Q J 8 5 3
♣ A J 8 4	♣ Q 5

Hand 2

♠ A K 9 8 6 4   ♠ Q J
♡ 7 4   ♡ A K 8
◇ K 4   ◇ A Q J 8 5 3
♣ K 8 2   ♣ Q 5

Hand 3

♠ K 10 8 6 4 2   ♠ Q J
♡ Q 7 4   ♡ A K 8
◇ K   ◇ A Q J 8 5 3
♣ A J 2   ♣ Q 5

Etc., etc., etc. So one cannot be faulted for simply jumping to six spades. In real life, that's what happened, but the sad story was that the whole deal actually was:

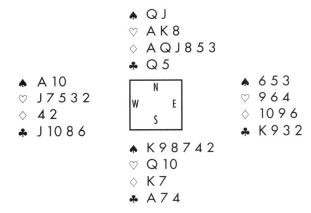

West had an easy club lead and the slam failed.

The situation could have been salvaged had North-South been using the Zia Cuebid.

When he first popularized this ploy (which had been used for many years by bridge experts, but sparingly), Zia would cuebid the suit he didn't want led, and then jump to slam. It got to the point where everyone led Zia's cuebid suit no matter what the rest of their hand was. So although it no longer works as a wily trick (although we suppose you could double-cross the opponents and cuebid your ace-queen to get that lead), the cuebid can still be used constructively if the partners are on the same wavelength. With the hand under discussion, the bidding could go:

West	North	East	South
			1♠
pass	2◇	pass	2♠
pass	3♣[1]		

1. Zia Cuebid.

If East passes rather than doubling for the lead, South goes ahead and bids six spades at his next opportunity, feeling sort of safe that a club won't be led. If East doubles 3♣, South bids as follows:

pass	no help in clubs (whereupon North signs off in 4♠)
redouble	second-round control, king or singleton
4♣	a re-cuebid, showing first-round control (whereupon North bids 6◊ or 6NT to protect his queen of clubs)

Zia Cuebids can be (and have been!) used on the way to game as well. For example, you hold:

♠ A K 9 7 5 3 2   ♡ 5 4   ◊ A Q 10   ♣ Q

You	Oppt	Partner	Oppt
1♠	pass	2♠	pass
3♡[1]	pass	any bid	pass
4♠	all pass		

1. Presumably natural, but if he forces to game himself, it might be lead-inhibiting!

THE ZIA CUEBID IN ACTION

This deal was reported by Howard Weinstein in the April 2001 ACBL *Bridge Bulletin*. Howard held this hand in the Cap Gemini tournament (he and partner Steve Garner finished second; Zia and Andrew Robson won for the second year in a row).

Here's the auction after which Howard's RHO had to lead from this hand against 6♡:

♠ A Q 9 7 5   ♡ K   ◊ 6 5 3   ♣ J 8 7 6

West	North	East	South
Weinstein		*Garner*	
		pass	pass
1◊	2♣	dbl	3♠
4♣	pass	4♡	pass
5♣	pass	5♡	pass
6♡	all pass		

Since his partner had twice failed to double Howard's club cuebids, South led the ♠A. Not a success! Here was the whole deal:

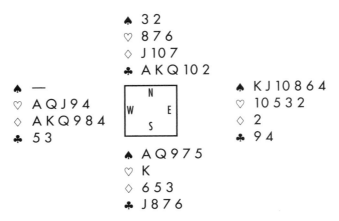

```
              ♠ 3 2
              ♡ 8 7 6
              ◇ J 10 7
              ♣ A K Q 10 2
♠ —                              ♠ K J 10 8 6 4
♡ A Q J 9 4       N              ♡ 10 5 3 2
◇ A K Q 9 8 4   W   E            ◇ 2
♣ 5 3             S              ♣ 9 4
              ♠ A Q 9 7 5
              ♡ K
              ◇ 6 5 3
              ♣ J 8 7 6
```

The South player had psyched against Howard's teammate at an earlier tournament, so Howard decided to give him a taste of his own medicine by cuebidding 4♣! His plan was that if North doubled, Steve Garner could pass (showing no club control) or redouble (showing first- or second-round control), and then Howard would know whether to bid slam or not. North knew exactly what Howard was trying to do (i.e., elicit information from his partner about clubs) so he ('the man who knew too much') refused to cooperate by doubling. Howard had no idea whether or not his partner possessed a club control when he bid 4♡, so he decided to try again, by bidding 5♣! Finally, having again failed to obtain any information about a club control, Howard decided just to bid slam and hope for the best. Bearing in mind the earlier hand, he must have felt that justice had been served!

Fine Arts Conventions

'Switch' and other Transfer-type Responses in Competition

62

PREVIEW

Look at this deal at IMPs, both vulnerable.

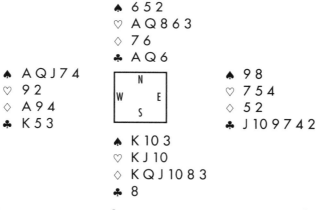

	♠ 6 5 2		
	♡ A Q 8 6 3		
	◇ 7 6		
	♣ A Q 6		

♠ A Q J 7 4   ♠ 9 8
♡ 9 2   ♡ 7 5 4
◇ A 9 4   ◇ 5 2
♣ K 5 3   ♣ J 10 9 7 4 2

      ♠ K 10 3
      ♡ K J 10
      ◇ K Q J 10 8 3
      ♣ 8

West	North	East	South
			1◇
1♠	2♡	pass	3♡
pass	4♡	all pass	

East leads a spade and the defense swiftly takes three spades and, later, the ace of diamonds. Your North-South result is -100. Are you satisfied with this score?

THE SOLUTION

Marty Bergen, Meckwell, and many other 'high-tech' bidders will reach four hearts from the South side — because they play **Switch** — and if you are unlucky enough to be playing against them, you will lose 13 IMPs.

How does Switch work? When your opponent overcalls your minor-suit opening with one spade, you switch the responses of the other two suits at the two-level.

Opener	Oppt	Responder	Oppt
1♢	1♠	?	

2♡   **by responder shows clubs**

2♣   **by responder shows hearts**

The advantage of switching is that you keep the overcaller on lead when you find a fit. The concept behind Switch is: keep the hand with the strength on opening lead. The idea of 'transferring' the play to the stronger hand is familiar to everyone because of Jacoby Transfers. But in Switch you don't transfer — you merely switch the missing two suits.

SWITCH PLUS

You can actually play Switch in all situations through the three-level! For example:

Opener	Oppt	Responder	Oppt
1♠	2♢	3♣[1]	
	1. Hearts.		

Opener	Oppt	Responder	Oppt
1♢	2♡	3♣[1]	
	1. Spades.		

Opener	Oppt	Responder	Oppt
1♣	1♡	2♢[1]	
	1. Spades.		

In the last auction, opener can bid 2♡ to say, 'I don't know what to bid at this point'.

If you play the standard variety Switch, you must know exactly what situations the invention applies to. But if you play **Switch Plus**, you have a simple formula for remembering:

Opener	Oppt	Responder	Oppt
any suit	overcall	Switch the other suits	

TRANSFERS AFTER TAKEOUT DOUBLES

A form of Switch can also be used after a takeout double, and is becoming quite popular.

West	North	East	South
			1♢
dbl	1♡		

North's bid shows spades. In this way, the strong hand, i.e., the takeout doubler, will be on lead:

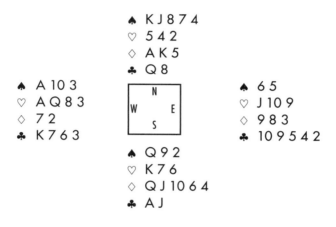

West	North	East	South
			1♢
dbl	?		

Four spades is cold from the South side, but fails by a trick when North declares and East leads the ♡J.

Some pairs play that a redouble shows hearts here. They give up the strength-showing redouble in order to be able to transfer to hearts. After 1♣–dbl, you can give up the one-diamond bid and play that 1♢ = hearts.

Sometimes you can direct a lead, and then show support, if given the opportunity:

♠ 5 2   ♡ J 6 3   ♢ A Q 10 8 4   ♣ 5 4 3

Partner	Oppt	You	Oppt
1♡	dbl	?	

Bid 2♣, transfer to 2♢, planning to support hearts next. If fourth seat bids spades, partner will know what to lead.

Preemptive Jumps after Partner Doubles their Artificial Bid

PREVIEW

What would you do with this hand at IMPs, neither side vulnerable?

♠ Q 9 6 2　♡ A K 10　◇ A K 4 2　♣ 8 4

Oppt	Partner	Oppt	You
1NT	pass	2◇[1]	?
	1. Transfer to hearts.		

Suppose you double. The bidding continues:

Oppt	Partner	Oppt	You
1NT	pass	2◇	dbl
2♡	4◇	4♡	?

What's going on here? It sounds like 4◇ is a preempt, because 1NT was strong. But exactly what does partner's hand look like? You now know that partner has at most two hearts (they accepted the transfer). If he has as little as queen-sixth of diamonds and ace- or king-fourth in clubs, with a singleton spade and two hearts, you've got five diamonds practically laydown, while they're (perhaps) making four hearts! On the other hand, something's fishy here. You've got a big hand and they're in game. Perhaps partner has a yarborough. Or perhaps your RHO is the one with a yarborough. Who has what? What should you bid? The choices are:

1) 5◇, to make　　　2) double　　　3) pass

SOLUTION

A very simple agreement can make your life easier: preemptive raises in competition show a willingness to defend at the level to which you preempted. This can mean one of two things:

1) I've preempted them to the four-level because I think we have a good chance to defeat them at the four-level;

2) I've preempted them to the four-level because I would like them to play at the four-level and not any higher!

Your partner, then, bid four diamonds because he either thinks your side has a chance to defeat them (and he doesn't know about your three trump honors!), or he's worried that they have a slam. Let's return to the hand in question and our possible calls. We have a game if partner has something like:

♠ 5   ♡ 6 4   ◇ Q 9 8 7 6 5   ♣ A 7 6 5

or even the same hand with ♣K765 because the ace rates to be onside.

Let's put ourselves in partner's position for a moment. Suppose you have this 6-4 hand and your partner doubled their two-diamond transfer, showing diamonds. What would you do? Would you bid 4◇? Do you fear they have a slam and you want to preempt them out of it? No, not really. You have no reason to suppose they've got a slam. Would you bid 4◇ because you'd like them to play in four hearts, believing you have a chance to defeat them there? No, you do not expect to defeat four hearts with this hand.

Therefore, you would not bid 4◇ with this hand. You would bid 5◇, thinking:

1) We might make 5◇.

2) They might take the push to 5♡ and go down.

3) They might propel themselves to 6♡ and go down (after all, I have that top club honor).

4) They might double us in five diamonds and we go down one or two while they make 4♡ (even if we go down three it's not the end of the world at IMPs).

5) We might go down in five diamonds when they can't make anything.

Since there is only the one bad scenario, you should bid 5◇ with six diamonds and a four-card side-suit.

Let's return to the hand from your original point of view:

♠ Q 9 6 2   ♡ A K 10   ◇ A K 4 2   ♣ 8 4

Oppt	Partner	Oppt	You
1NT	pass	2◇	dbl
2♡	4◇	4♡	?

We have deduced that bidding 5◇ to make is out. That leaves us with a choice between pass and double. Partner either has two tricks or so, i.e., he pushed them to the four-level because he thinks your side has a good shot to defeat 4♡, or he has a yarborough and wanted to take away all of their slam-investigation room. Is there any way to figure out which it is? Not really, but one thing is for sure: if you double them, they are not going to redouble because they are missing the ace-king-ten of trumps and at least 16 high-card points. If partner has the hand with a couple of tricks, they may be going for a big number. The possible big pickup is worth the risk, so we double. The whole deal is:

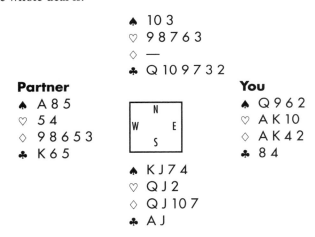

and we pick up a nice 300 penalty.

To sum up: after you double their Stayman or Transfer bid, partner's preempt is not a game invitation (with a good fit with you and a good playing hand, he either bids game himself or cuebids). It shows a desire to have the opponents play at the level he's bid to. (You can apply this idea to other situations where a preempt is made in the middle of the opponents' auction.)

Undercalls Over 1♣

You pick up at favorable vulnerability:

♠ A Q J 8 7 3   ♡ 4 3 2   ◇ J 8 7   ♣ A

Partner holds:

♠ K 10 9 5   ♡ K 9 6   ◇ A 9 3 2   ♣ J 5

Your RHO opens the bidding one club. What contract do you want to reach?

THE SOLUTION

As in many other situations, it can be advantageous to get the strong opposing hand on lead. The answer is to use Undercalls in this auction. This convention, which almost nobody plays, is lots of fun and can produce terrific swings in your favor!

The convention applies only after a one-club opening bid. In second seat, your one-level overcall is one under your suit:

Oppt		You	Oppt	Partner
1♣		?		
1◇	=	hearts		
1♡	=	spades		
1♠	=	diamonds		

That's all there is to it, basically.
There are four things you gain:

1) **You get partner to declare the hand in your long suit, putting the opening bidder on opening lead. The advantage of having the opening lead come from the stronger hand is an established fact.**

2) **You get to make two bids (usually) for the price of one, since most of the time partner will bid your suit or something else and you get to make another bid (standard transfer advantage).**

3) **You escape a penalty double if partner happens to hold length in the suit you bid and shortness in the suit you've shown.**

4) **With diamonds you preempt their one-level by overcalling 1♠.**

The full deal related to our preview was:

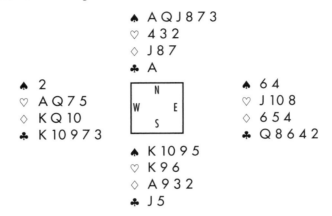

```
              ♠ A Q J 8 7 3
              ♡ 4 3 2
              ◊ J 8 7
              ♣ A
  ♠ 2                        ♠ 6 4
  ♡ A Q 7 5        N         ♡ J 10 8
  ◊ K Q 10      W     E      ◊ 6 5 4
  ♣ K 10 9 7 3     S         ♣ Q 8 6 4 2
              ♠ K 10 9 5
              ♡ K 9 6
              ◊ A 9 3 2
              ♣ J 5
```

At every table, North declared a spade partscore or game and made either eight or nine tricks after East led the jack of hearts. Playing undercalls, the auction goes:

West	North	East	South
1♣	1♡	pass	2♠
pass	3♣	pass	4♠
all pass			

West leads the king of diamonds. South wins the ace, cashes the ace of clubs, leads a trump to hand and ruffs a club, draws a second trump and leads a diamond toward dummy: end of hand. A heart is discarded on the thirteenth diamond. If West started with two diamonds, he is endplayed. If West started with four diamonds, he gets out with a diamond and declarer wins the jack, leads a third trump to hand and plays a diamond, throwing a heart. Now West is endplayed. Four spades, bid and made — but from the South side only.

It's true that even if South plays the hand, a club or spade lead will defeat 4♠, but only if West defends perfectly. After winning the first round of diamonds, he must shift to a heart, away from his AQxx. It's not easy!

WHAT DO YOU LOSE BY PLAYING UNDERCALLS?

You lose the ability to hear partner bid 1♡ or 1♠ as he could after a natural 1◇ overcall. Also, since you must overcall 1♠ with diamonds, committing your side to the two-level, you'll need a better diamond suit than for a normal 1◇ overcall.

The XYZ Convention*

Opener	**Responder**
♠ A 3 2	♠ K
♡ A 6 4 3	♡ K 8 2
◇ A 5	◇ K 7 6 3 2
♣ Q 7 6 4	♣ A K 8 2

1♣	1◇
1♡	?

Auctions that begin this way can get very awkward; most players would have to continue by using a fourth-suit forcing jump to 2♠. Is there a better way?

*This convention was developed by Joe Kivel

THE XYZ CONVENTION

After the sequence by two partners (with or without interference) of

Opener	Responder
1x	1y
1z	?

(x, y, and z represent any call other than pass by the partnership at the one-level) responder has the following choices:

2♣   **asks opener to bid 2◇; responder may pass 2◇ or make an invitational bid.**

2◇   **shows a game-forcing hand, with various contracts in mind.**

2♡/2♠   **weak, unless it is a reverse.**

2NT   **invitational.**

3♣   **signoff.**

3◇/3♡/3♠   **game-forcing.**

If the opponents do not interfere, there are ten possible XYZ sequences:

Opener	Responder
1♣	1◇
1♡	

Opener	Responder
1♣	1◇
1♠	

Opener	Responder
1♣	1◇
1NT	

Opener	Responder
1♣	1♡
1♠	

Opener	Responder
1♣	1♡
1NT	

Opener	Responder
1♣	1♠
1NT	

Opener	Responder
1♢	1♡
1♠	

Opener	Responder
1♢	1♡
1NT	

Opener	Responder
1♢	1♠
1NT	

Opener	Responder
1♡	1♠
1NT	

But if the opponents come in, there are many others, for example:

Opener	Oppt	Responder	Oppt
1♣	dbl	redbl	1♡
1♠			

Opener	Oppt	Responder	Oppt
1♢	1♡	dbl	pass
1NT			

Opener	Oppt	Responder	Oppt
1♢	pass	1♡	1♠
dbl[1]			

1. When this is a support double, it counts as z, the third call in the XYZ formula.

Some examples

One advantage of XYZ is that it gives you the ability to stay below the three-level in invitational partscore bidding, e.g.

Opener	Responder
♠ A J 5 4	♠ Q 7 3 2
♡ 6 4 2	♡ A Q 7 5
◇ K J 7 3	◇ 4 2
♣ A 8	♣ K 7 5
1◇	1♡
1♠	2♣[1]
2◇	2♠[2]
pass	

1. Forces 2◇.
2. Invitational.

Standard bidding leads to a 3♠ contract, which is in jeopardy with any bad break.

Opener	Responder
♠ A 5 4 3	♠ K 6 2
♡ A 2	♡ K Q J 5 4
◇ K 7	◇ J 10 6 2
♣ Q 8 6 5 4	♣ 2
1♣	1♡
1♠	2♣[1]
2◇	2♡[2]
pass	

1. Forces 2◇.
2. Invitational.

Another advantage is that the 2◇ rebid after XYZ bidding gives you room to find your fit (or non-fit) and probe for slam. The responding hand below is from our preview:

Opener	Responder
♠ A 3 2	♠ K
♡ A 6 4 3	♡ K 8 2
◇ A 5	◇ K 7 6 3 2
♣ Q 7 6 4	♣ A K 8 2

Opener	Responder
1♣	1◇
1♡	2◇[1]
2NT	3♣
3◇	3♡
3♠	4♣
4♡	6♣
pass	

1. Game-force.

After West rebids 2NT, denying diamond support or a 4-card spade suit and limiting his hand, he gets to make three cuebids (3◇, 3♠, 4♡)! This is an interesting play hand as well. West should try to set up the dummy, draw trumps if they are 3-2, then ruff a diamond, as long as they're not 5-1.

QUESTIONS AND ANSWERS

1) After 2♣, can opener bid something other than 2◇?

Yes. Responder might be planning to pass 2◇, so if opener would have bid again opposite a Standard weak 2◇ rebid by responder, he must immediately make that bid. For example, if opener has:

♠ A K 6 5   ♡ K 4 3 2   ◇ 2   ♣ A 9 7 5 4

1♣	1♡
1♠	2♣[1]
2♡	

1. Forces 2◇.

Opener does not want to play 2◇ if responder has hearts and diamonds and a weak hand.

2) What is the difference between 1x-1y; 1z-2NT and going through 2♣ and then bidding 2NT?

Use the 2♣ sequence to show a hand that has the appropriate point count but offers a choice of contracts, e.g., some type of 5-4-3-1 hand or other semi-unbalanced hand.

3) What's the difference between responder's second-round jump to 3◇ or higher and going through 2◇ (game-force) first?

1x-1y; 1z-3y/3z is forcing, for example:

Opener	Responder
1♣	1♡
1♠	3♡

showing an excellent suit, whereas the sequence

Opener	Responder
1♣	1♡
1♠	2◇
2NT	3♡

shows a six-card suit but offers a choice between alternative contracts.

1) Using the 2♣ relay gives up the ability to play 2♣.

2) Occasionally an opponent will double 2♣ or 2◇ as a lead-director.

Yellow Rose of Texas

66

PREVIEW

You pick up:

♠ 6 5 3   ♡ K 7 2   ◇ A 8 4 3   ♣ A Q 2

Partner opens 2NT. What is your response?

YELLOW ROSE OF TEXAS

The convention is used after partner opens 1NT or 2NT if you also use Texas Transfers. As responder, you hold a hand that looks like a 6NT bid, but instead you show your hand pattern to partner, in case you (1) don't belong in slam because of duplication, or (2) belong in a suit contract instead of 6NT. The convention is more useful at IMPs than at matchpoints, where a slightly risky 6NT may be worth the extra matchpoints.

To use **Yellow Rose of Texas***, you respond Texas: 4◇, 4♡, or 4♠. All of these bids are transfers (4♠ transfers to 4NT), but don't actually promise the next suit. After partner takes the transfer, you bid again, saying, 'Partner, I don't have a long suit — I have a 6NT bid with some 4-3-3-3 or 4-4-3-2 shape. Here is my pattern:

---

*This convention is one of more than 200 invented by the prolific Danny Kleinman

Partner	You
1NT	4◇
4♡	4♠/5♣/5♡[1]

1. Doubleton diamond and tripleton in suit bid.

Partner	You
1NT	4♡
4♠	5♣/5◇/5♠[1]

1. Doubleton heart and tripleton in suit bid.

Partner	You
1NT	4♠
4NT	5♣/5◇/5♡[1]

1. Doubleton spade and tripleton in suit bid.

Partner	You
1NT	4◇
4♡	5◇[1]

1. Doubleton club and tripleton diamond.

Partner	You
1NT	4♡
4♠	5♡[1]

1. Doubleton club and tripleton heart.

Partner	You
1NT	4♠
4NT	5♠[1]

1. Doubleton club and tripleton spade.

Formula

If you bid two suits, you have a doubleton in the first one and a tripleton in the second. If you bid and rebid the same suit, you have a doubleton club and tripleton in the suit you bid twice. Notice that responder never bids a suit in which he has four cards, and opener doesn't show a suit until he's ready to suggest a final contract. Thus only dummy's, not declarer's, hand pattern is revealed to the defenders.

Another note: Texas followed by 4NT is still Keycard Blackwood with the suit transferred to as the trump suit.

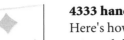

4333 hands

Here's how you show 4333 patterns. With a 4-card major, transfer to it and then rebid 5NT. With a 4-card diamond suit, bid 4♠ then 5NT. With four clubs, start with 4◇ and rebid 5♠.

All these 4333 or 4432 hands include enough points for slam, but no more than that; for example, about 17 or 18 points opposite a 15-17 one notrump.

OPENER'S ACTIONS

Opener may now sign off in any contract. There's usually no further science at this point.

The following examples are based on 15-17 1NT openings and 20-22 2NT openings.

Opener	Responder
♠ A K 4	♠ Q J 6 3
♡ 7 2	♡ A K 4
◇ A 6 5 4	◇ K 2
♣ A 5 4 2	♣ K J 7 6

1NT	4◇
4♡	5♡[1]
6♣	pass

1. 4-3-2-4 shape.

On these cards 6♣ is a much, much better slam than 6NT.

Let's look at our preview hand:

♠ 6 5 3   ♡ K 7 2   ◇ A 8 4 3   ♣ A Q 2

Partner opens 2NT. What is your response?

Before you learned about Yellow Rose of Texas, would you dream of anything but 6NT? However:

Opener	Responder
♠ A K	♠ 6 5 3
♡ A 4 3	♡ K 7 2
◇ K Q J 2	◇ A 8 4 3
♣ K 6 5 4	♣ A Q 2

2NT	4♠
4NT	5NT[1]
6◇	pass

1. 3-3-4-3 shape.

6NT depends on a 3-3 club break, but 6◇ is practically cold.

Opener	Responder
♠ K Q 5	♠ A 10 7
♡ A J 3	♡ K Q 6
◇ K Q 2	◇ A J 5
♣ J 8 7 4	♣ K 10 5 3

1NT	4◇
4♡	5♠[1]
5NT	pass

1. 3-3-3-4.

When West learns about the mirror distribution, he signs off in 5NT. Even this may be too high! With the ten of clubs included, eleven tricks are likely, but if not, a little luck will produce eleven tricks anyway. In either case, the horrible 6NT was avoided. Switch the queen of hearts into the club suit and 6NT requires a 3-2 club break and heart finesse -- not so bad, but still below 50%.

Opener	Responder
♠ A K 4 3	♠ 7 5 2
♡ K 8	♡ A Q J 6
◇ A 4 3	◇ K 7
♣ J 8 6 3	♣ A K 5 4

1NT	4◇
4♡	4♠[1]
5♣	6♣
pass	

1. 3-4-2-4 shape.

Here there's space for some cooperation. Opener learns about the 4-4 club fit and doubleton diamond, but hedges with 5♣, because of his poor trumps. Responder, with great trumps and prime values, bids six.

Opener	Responder
♠ A K 4	♠ Q 8 5 2
♡ A K 5	♡ J 3
◇ K J 7 6 3	◇ A 4 2
♣ K 8	♣ A 6 4 2

2NT	4♡
4♠	5◇[1]
6◇	pass

1. 4-2-3-4 shape.

This time opener discovers the 5-3 diamond fit.

Note (for advanced Yellow Rose partnerships!):
Over 2NT, many play that Texas is slam invitational (whereas Jacoby transfer followed by a raise to game is a signoff) — an excellent way to play (see page 19). If you play this way, and also want to use Yellow Rose, you'll have to use a special rebid over Texas, such as 2NT-4◇-4♠ to show that opener accepts the slam invitation (opposite a normal Texas); now responder will bid one step (4NT) to say he has long hearts, while any other bid will be Yellow Rose.

In the last example above, opener would bid 4NT over 4♡, saying he accepts if his partner is inviting slam with six spades, and now 5♣ by responder (one step) would show long spades (then opener can ask for keycards with the next step, for example). On the hands shown, responder would not bid 5♣, but bid 5◇, saying he had Yellow Rose, not a Texas transfer (if responder had Yellow Rose with two hearts and three clubs, he would have to bid 6♣).

WHAT DO YOU LOSE BY PLAYING YELLOW ROSE OF TEXAS?

1) Some play that Texas followed by a new suit is Exclusion Keycard Blackwood with a void in the second suit bid by responder. You can't use this convention if you're using Yellow Rose.

2) You might tip off the opening leader when you reveal your pattern. For example, suppose you use Yellow Rose and partner chooses to play in 6NT. The opening leader holds ◇ 10932 and ♣ 10974. He was about to lead a club, until he heard about dummy holding two diamonds and four clubs. So he leads a diamond instead.

Fine Arts Conventions